WANDERING SPIRITS

Peace goes into the making of a poet as flour goes into the making of bread.

Pablo Neruda

For as long as I can remember I've been fascinated by South America. The dramatic landscapes, exuberant cultures and powerful mythologies have always thrilled and inspired me, a colourful contrast to the grim and grey backdrop of the northern UK town where I grew up. The strong awareness and respect for the supernatural world of spirits is ever apparent, and never more so than in Chile. This giant jigsaw of the most beautiful elements of the natural world, with its turbulent past and unique history has long-inspired artists, poets, writers and artisans. The magical realism of Isabel Allende and

Pablo Neruda's work provides a glimpse of the rich vein of spirituality running through Chilean life.

Join me in *Wandering Spirits* on a personal journey through Chile. There are designs to appeal to fashion-conscious knitters of all ages and knitting expertise – a diverse collection bound together by a sprinkling of Chilean magic.

Love, laughter and great knitting always,

MAR

BAHIA
pattern page 36

DUNE
pattern page 38

SURF
pattern page 40

PLAYA
pattern page 44

LAGOON
pattern page 46

CASA

FIREFLY
pattern page 50

INES
pattern page 52

CORBATA
pattern page 55

DESERT ROSE
pattern page 56

CRUZ
pattern page 60

MONTANA

LAVA
pattern page 64

BOLA
pattern page 67

ROCCO
pattern page 68

CALDERA
pattern page 70

BARRANCO
pattern page 72

ATACAMA
pattern page 74

BAHIA page 36   DUNE page 38   SURF page 40   CAYO page 42

FIREFLY page 50   INES page 52   CORBATA page 55   DESERT ROSE page 56

LAVA page 64   BOLA page 67   ROCCO page 68   CALDERA page 70

MAR

CASA

MONTANA

DESIGN GALLERY

MAR
PATTERNS

Bahia

SIZES

XS   to fit bust 32in/81.25cm
S   to fit bust 34in/86.25cm
M   to fit bust 36in/91.5cm
L   to fit bust 38in/96.5cm
XL   to fit bust 40in/101.5cm
XXL to fit bust 42in/106.5cm
See schematic for actual
measurements

MATERIALS

Araucania Patagonia:
5 (5, 5, 6, 6, 6) skeins
PT714/KFI-233
0.25in/7mm ribbon 10yds/9m
One pair each 5mm (US 8)
and 5.5mm (US 9) needles or
size to obtain tension
Tapestry needle
Stitch holders

TENSION

15 sts and 20 rows =
4in/10cms over stocking
stitch.

STITCHES

Garter stitch
Stocking stitch
See Information page 76

BACK

Using smaller ndles, cast on 62 (66, 70, 74, 78, 82) sts and work 1.25in/3cm in garter st. Change to larger ndles and work in st st. to end. When work measures 2in/5cm from c.o.e. ending on WS row, **work shaping**:

XS & S   dec 1 st at both ends of next, then ev foll 12th row twice – 56 (60) sts.

M & L   ec 1 st at both ends of next, then ev foll 13th row twice – 64 (68) sts.

XL & XXL dec 1 st at both ends of next, then ev foll 14th row twice – 72 (76) sts.

Cont as set until work measures 7 (7, 7.5, 7.5, 8, 8)in/ 17.75 (19, 19, 20.25, 20.25)cm from c.o.e. ending on WS row, then inc as foll:

XS & S   inc 1 st at both ends of next, then ev foll 11th row twice – 62 (66) sts.

M & L   inc 1 st at both ends of next, then ev foll 10th row twice – 70 (74) sts.

XL & XXL inc 1 st at both ends of next, then ev foll 9th row twice – 78 (82) sts.

Cont until work measures 14.5in/37cm from c.o.e. ending on WS row, then **shape armhole**:

Cast off 4 (5, 6, 7, 8, 9) sts at beg of next 2 rows – 54 (56, 58, 60, 62, 64) sts.

Cont as set until work measures 21.25 (21.25, 21.75, 21.75, 22.25, 22.25)in/54 (54, 55.25, 55.25, 56.5, 56.5)cm from c.o.e. ending on a WS row, then **shape neck and shoulder**:

Next row (RS) Work 18 (18, 19, 19, 20, 20) sts, place centre 18(20, 20, 22, 22, 24) sts on holder, join a second ball of yarn and work to end. Working both sides at the same time, dec1 st at both neck edges on next and foll alt row.

At the same time work and place 5 (5, 5, 5, 6, 6) sts on holder at armhole edge on next row, (for left back neck it will be foll row), and 5 (5, 6, 6, 6, 6) sts on foll alt row.
Cast off over full 16 (16, 17, 17, 18, 18) sts.

FRONT

Work as for back until work measures 11.5in/29.25cm from c.o.e. ending on WS row, then begin **neck shaping**:

Divide the sts in two, work the first half, then join a second ball of yarn and work to end. Working both sides at the same time, dec as foll, keeping side edge incs correct:

XS   1 st at neck edge on next, then ev foll 4th row 6 times, then ev foll 5th row 4 times – 16 sts

S   1 st at neck edge on next, then ev foll 4th row 11 times – 16 sts

M   1 st at neck edge on next, then ev foll 4th row 9 times, then ev foll 5th row twice – 17 sts

L   1 st at neck edge on next, then ev foll 3rd row twice, then ev foll 4th row 10 times – 17 sts

XL   1 st at neck edge on next, then ev foll 4th row 11 times, then ev foll 5th row once – 18 sts

XXL 1 st at neck edge on next, then ev foll 3rd row 3 times, then ev foll 4th row 10 times – 18 sts

At the same time when work measures 14.5in/37cm from c.o.e ending on WS row, **shape armhole**:

Cast off 4 (5, 6, 7, 8, 9) sts at beg of next 2 rows.

Cont as set until work measures 21.25 (21.25, 21.75, 21.75, 22.25, 22.25)in/54 (54, 55.25, 55.25, 56.5, 56.5)cm from c.o.e. ending on a WS row, then **shape shoulder**:

Work and place 5 (5, 5, 5, 6, 6) sts on holder at armhole edge on next row, (for second side it will be on foll row), then work and place 5 (5, 6, 6, 6, 6) sts on holder on foll alt row.

Cast off over full 16 (16, 17, 17, 18, 18) sts.

FINISHING
Join right shoulder seam.

Neckband
Using smaller ndles, with RS facing and starting at left shoulder, pick up and k 42 (42, 44, 44, 46, 46) sts down left front neck, 42 (42, 44, 44, 46, 46) sts up right front neck edge, 2 sts down left back neck, 18 (20, 20, 22, 22, 24) sts from holder at centre back and 2 sts up right back – 106 (108, 112, 114, 118, 120) sts. Work 2 rows in garter st. Cast off knitwise.
Join left shoulder seam.

Armbands
Using smaller ndles, with RS facing, pick up and k4 (5, 6, 7, 8, 9) sts along horizontal edge, 56 (56, 60, 60, 64, 64) sts evenly around armhole and a further 4 (5, 6, 7, 8, 9) sts along horizontal edge at other side – 64 (66, 72, 74, 80, 82) sts.

Work 2 rows in garter st, then cast off knitwise.
Join side seams and armbands in one line.
Work 1 row of blanket stitch around neck and armbands.

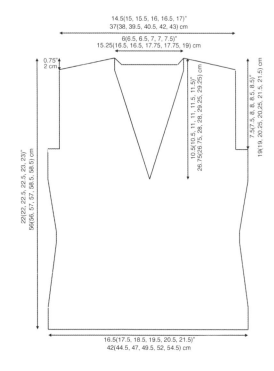

14.5(15, 15.5, 16, 16.5, 17)"
37(38, 39.5, 40.5, 42, 43) cm

6(6.5, 6.5, 7, 7, 7.5)"
15.25(16.5, 16.5, 17.75, 17.75, 19) cm

0.75"
2 cm

10.5(10.5, 11, 11, 11.5, 11.5)"
26.75(26.75, 28, 28, 29.25, 29.25) cm

7.5(7.5, 8, 8, 8.5, 8.5)"
19(19, 20.25, 20.25, 21.5, 21.5) cm

22(22, 22.5, 22.5, 23, 23)"
56(56, 57, 57, 58.5, 58.5) cm

16.5(17.5, 18.5, 19.5, 20.5, 21.5)"
42(44.5, 47, 49.5, 52, 54.5) cm

Dune

SIZES
XS   to fit bust 32in/ 81.25cm
S   to fit bust 34in/ 86.25cm
M   to fit bust 36in/ 91.5cm
L   to fit bust 38in/ 96.5cm
XL   to fit bust 40in/ 101.5cm
XXL to fit bust 42in/ 106.5cm
See schematic for actual
measurements

MATERIALS
Araucania Chacabuco:
3 skeins PT732/KFI-757
One pair each 4.5mm (US 7)
and 5mm (US 8) needles *or
size to obtain tension*
Stitch holders and markers
2 x 34mm buttons

TENSION
14 sts and 24 rows = 4in/10
cms over stocking stitch

STITCHES
Garter stitch
Stocking stitch
Cable cast-on
See Information page 76

BACK
Using smaller ndles, cast on 58 (62, 64, 68, 72, 76) sts and work 1.25in/3cm in garter st, ending on WS row. Change to larger ndles and cont in st st until work measures 8.5in/21.5cm from c.o.e., ending on WS row, then **work armband:**
Next row (RS)   k
Next row   k5, purl to last 5 sts, k5
Repeat these two rows to end
When work measures 15.25 (15.25, 15.75, 15.75, 16.25, 16.25)in/38.75 (38.75, 40, 40, 41.25, 41.25)cm from c.o.e., ending on WS row,

shape shoulder and neck:
Next row (RS)   Work 19 (21, 21, 23, 24, 26) sts, place centre 20 (20, 22, 22, 24, 24) sts on holder, join a second ball of yarn and work to end. Working both sides at the same time, dec 1 st at both neck edges on next and foll alt row.
At the same time work and place 5 (6, 6, 7, 7, 8) sts on holder at armhole edge on next row, (for left back neck it will be foll row), and 6 (6, 6, 7, 7, 8) sts on foll alt row. Cast off over all 17 (19, 19, 21, 22, 24) sts.

LEFT FRONT
Using smaller ndles, cast on 19 (20, 21, 22, 23, 24) sts and work 1.25in/3 cm in garter st, ending on WS row. Change to larger ndles and cont as foll:
Next row (RS)   k
Next row   k5, p to end
Repeat these 2 rows until work measures 8.5in/ 21.5cm from c.o.e., ending on WS row, then **work armband:**
Next row (RS)   k
Next row   k5, purl to last 5 sts, k5
At the same time when work measures 8.5

(8.5, 9, 9, 9.5, 9.5)in/ 21.5 (21.5, 23, 23, 24, 24)cm from c.o.e., ending on RS row, cast on 17 (18, 18, 19, 20, 21) sts at beg of next row using cable cast-on, then work to end – 36 (38, 39, 41, 43, 45) sts.
Next row (RS)   k
Next row   k22 (23, 23, 24, 25, 26),
                   p to last 5 sts, k5.
Rep these 2 rows to end. When work measures 12.5 (12.5, 13, 13, 13,5, 13.5)in/31.75 (31.75, 33, 33, 34.25, 34.25)cm from c.o.e., ending on RS row, **shape neckline:**
Keeping patt correct as set, cast off 11 (11, 12, 12, 13, 13) sts at beg of next row. Then dec 1 st at neck edge on ev row 8 times – 17 (19, 19, 21, 22, 24) sts.
Continue in patt as set until work measures 15.25 (15.25, 15.75, 15.75, 16.25, 16.25)in/38.75 (38.75, 40, 40, 41.25, 41.25)cm from c.o.e., ending on WS row, then **shape shoulder:**
Work and place 5 (6, 6, 7, 7, 8) sts on holder at armhole edge on next row, (for left back neck it will be foll row), and 6 (6, 6, 7, 7, 8) sts on foll alt row.
Cast off over all 17 (19, 19, 21, 22, 24) sts.

RIGHT FRONT
As left front reversing all shapings and garter st bands. Insert buttonhole when work measures 9.5 (9.5, 10, 10, 10.5, 10.5)in/ 24 (24, 25.5, 25.5, 26.5, 26.5)cm from c.o.e. ending on WS row as foll:
Work 3 sts in patt as set, cast off 3 sts, work to end in patt. Cast on these sts when you come to them on next row.

FINISHING
Join shoulder seams

Neckband

With RS facing and using smaller ndles, starting at right centre front pick up and k11 (11, 12, 12, 13, 13) sts along straight edge of neck, 10 sts up right neck edge, 2 sts down right back neck edge, 20 (20, 22, 22, 24, 24) sts from holder at centre back, 2 sts up left back neck edge, 10 sts down left neck edge and k11 (11, 12, 12, 13, 13) sts along straight edge of left front neck edge – 66 (66, 70, 70, 74, 74) sts.

Work 1.5in/3.75cm in garter st, then cast off.

At the same time work buttonhole as before, starting on a RS row when neckband measures 0.75in/2cm.

Join side seams to point where armbands start. Attach two buttons on buttonband opposite buttonholes.

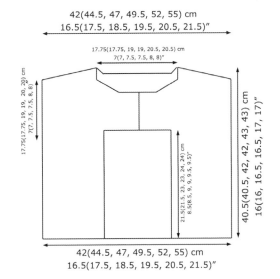

42(44.5, 47, 49.5, 52, 55) cm
16.5(17.5, 18.5, 19.5, 20.5, 21.5)"

17.75(17.75, 19, 19, 20.5, 20.5) cm
7(7, 7.5, 7.5, 8, 8)"

17.75(17.75, 19, 19, 20, 20) cm
7(7, 7.5, 7.5, 8, 8)"

40.5(40.5, 42, 42, 43, 43) cm
16(16, 16.5, 16.5, 17, 17)"

21.5(21.5, 23, 23, 24, 24) cm
8.5(8.5, 9, 9, 9.5, 9.5)"

42(44.5, 47, 49.5, 52, 55) cm
16.5(17.5, 18.5, 19.5, 20.5, 21.5)"

Surf

SIZES

XS   to fit chest 38in/96cm
S   to fit chest 40in/101cm
M   to fit chest 42in/106cm
L   to fit chest 44in/111cm
XL   to fit chest 46in/116cm
XXL   to fit chest 48in/122cm
See schematic for actual
measurements

MATERIALS

Araucania Pomaire:
2 (2, 2, 2, 3, 3) skeins
PT634/KFI-07 (A)
2 (2, 2, 2, 2, 2) skeins
PT699/KFI-67 (B)
One pair each 4mm (US 6)
and 4.5mm (US 7) *or size to
obtain tension*
One 4mm (US 6) circular
needle
One 4.5mm (US 7) circular
needle
Stitch holders

TENSION

18 sts and 26 rows =
4in/10cms over stocking stitch

STITCHES

1 x 1 rib
Stocking stitch
See Information page 76
Stripe pattern
Rows 1 & 2   Work in B
Rows 3 & 4   Work in A

BACK

Using smaller ndles and A, cast on 89 (93, 99, 103, 107, 113) sts and work 2in/5cm in 1 x 1 rib, Change to larger ndles and refer to stripe patt and rep to end in st st.
Cont until work measures 16 (16, 16.5, 16.5, 17, 17)in/40.5 (40.5, 42, 42, 43, 43)cm from c.o.e. ending on a WS row and then **shape armhole:**
Cast off 4 (4, 4, 5, 5, 5) sts at beg of next 2 rows. Then dec 1 st at both ends of next and every alt row 7 (8, 11, 11, 13, 15) times – 67 (69, 69, 71, 71, 73) sts.
Cont keeping stripe patt correct as set until work measures 24.5 (24.5, 25.5, 25.5, 26.5, 26.5)in/62.25 (62.25, 64.75, 64.75, 67/5, 67.5)cm from c.o.e. ending on a WS row, then **shape neck and shoulder:**
Next row (RS) Work 22sts, place centre 23 (25, 25, 27, 27, 29) sts on holder, join a second ball of yarn and work to end. Working both sides at the same time, dec1 st at both neck edges on next and foll alt row.
At the same time work and place 6 sts on holder at armhole edge on next row, (for left back neck it will be foll row), and 7 sts on foll alt row. Cast off over full 20 sts.

FRONT

Work as for back until work measures 17 (17, 17.5, 17.5, 18, 18)in/43 (43, 44.5, 44.5, 45.75, 45.75)cm from c.o.e. ending on WS row.
Then *at the same time* as armhole shaping, begin **neck shaping:**
Work to centre st and place it on holder, then join a second ball of yarn and work to end. Working both sides at the same time, dec as foll:

XS   1 st at neck edge on next, then ev foll 3rd row 9 times, then ev foll 4th row 3 times – 20sts

S   1 st at neck edge on next, then ev foll 3rd row 13 times – 20sts

M   1 st at neck edge on next, then ev foll 3rd row 11 times, then ev foll 4th row twice – 20sts

L   1 st at neck edge on next, then ev foll 3rd row 14 times – 20sts

XL   1 st at neck edge on next, then ev foll 3rd row 13 times, then ev foll 4th row once – 20sts

XXL   1 st at neck edge on next, then ev foll alt row twice, then ev foll 3rd row 13 times – 20sts

Cont in stripe patt as set until work measures 24.5 (24.5, 25.5, 25.5, 26.5, 26.5)in/62.25 (62.25, 64.75, 64.75, 67/5, 67.5)cm from c.o.e. ending on a WS row, then **shape shoulder:**
Work and place 6 sts on holder at armhole edge on next row, (for second side it will be on foll row), then work and place 7 sts on holder on foll **alt** row.
Cast off over full 20 sts.

FINISHING

Join right shoulder seam.
Neckband
Using smaller ndles and A, with RS facing and starting at left shoulder, pick up and k 40 (40, 42, 42, 45, 45) sts down left front neck, k1 from holder at centre front, 40 (40, 42, 42, 45, 45) sts up right front neck edge, 2 sts down left back neck, 23 (25, 25, 27, 27, 29) sts from holder at centre back and 2 sts up right back – 108 (110, 114, 114, 122, 124) sts. Work 2 rows in 1 x 1 rib, dec 1 st at both sides of centre front st on every

row, keeping rib correct.

Cast off in rib. Join left shoulder seam.

Armbands

Using smaller ndles and A, with RS facing, pick up and k94 (94, 100, 100, 106, 106) sts evenly around armhole edge. Work 2 rows in 1 x 1 rib, then cast off in rib.

Join side seams and armbands in one line.

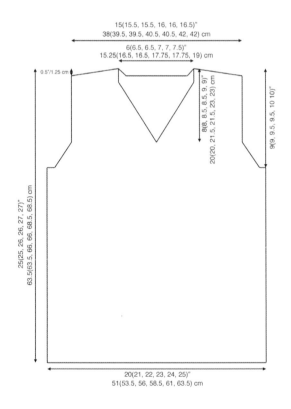

15(15.5, 15.5, 16, 16, 16.5)"
38(39.5, 39.5, 40.5, 40.5, 42, 42) cm

6(6.5, 6.5, 7, 7, 7.5)"
15.25(16.5, 16.5, 17.75, 17.75, 19) cm

0.5"/1.25 cm

8(8, 8.5, 8.5, 9, 9)"
20(20, 21.5, 21.5, 23, 23) cm

9(9, 9.5, 9.5, 10 10)"

25(25, 26, 26, 27, 27)"
63.5(63.5, 66, 66, 68.5, 68.5) cm

20(21, 22, 23, 24, 25)"
51(53.5, 56, 58.5, 61, 63.5) cm

Cayo

SIZES

XS to fit bust 32in/ 81.25cm,
    hips 34in/ 86.25cm
S   to fit bust 34in/ 86.25cm,
    hips 36in/ 91.5cm
M   to fit bust 36in/ 91.5cm,
    hips 38in/ 96.5cm
L   to fit bust 38in/ 96.5cm,
    hips 40in/101.5cm
XL to fit bust 40in/101.5cm,
    hips 42in/ 106.5cm
XXL to fit bust 42in/106.5cm,
    hips 44in/111.5cm
See schematic for actual
measurements

MATERIALS

Araucania Pomaire:
4 (4, 4, 5, 5, 5) skeins
PT635/KFI-08
One pair each 4mm (US 6)
and 4.5mm (US 7) needles or
size to obtain tension
4mm (US 6) circular needle
4.5mm (US 7) crochet hook
Stitch holders and markers

TENSION

18 sts and 26 rows =
4in/10cms over stocking
stitch

BACK

Using smaller ndles, cast on 76 (80, 86, 90, 94, 100) sts and work 2in/5cm in openwork stitch, ending on WS row. Change to larger ndles and cont as foll:

Next row (RS)   (yrn, p2tog) 3 times, k to last 6 sts, (yrn, p2tog) 3 times

Next row   (yrn, p2tog) 3 times, p to last 6 sts, (yrn, p2tog) 3 times

Repeat these two rows until work measures 9.5 (9.5,10, 10, 10.5, 10.5)in/ 24 (24, 25.5, 25.5, 26.75, 26.75)cm from c.o.e., ending on WS row. Cont in st st to end dec 1 st at both ends of 35th(35th, 33rd, 33rd, 33rd, 33rd) row, then again on foll 34th row – 72 (76, 82, 86, 90, 96) sts. Cont until work measures 25.5in/64.75cm from c.o.e., ending on WS row, then **shape armhole:**
Cast off 5 (5, 5, 6, 6, 7) sts at beg of next 2 rows. Then dec 1 st at both ends of next and ev alt row 6 (8, 8, 9, 9, 11) times – 50 (50, 56, 56, 60, 60) sts. ***
When work measures 28.5 (28.5, 29, 29, 29.5, 29.5)in/ 72.25 (72.25, 73.5, 73.5, 75, 75)cm from c.o.e., ending on WS row,
shape neckline:

Next row (RS)   Work 17 (17, 19, 19, 20, 20) sts as set, place 16 (16, 18, 18, 20, 20) sts on holder, join a second ball of yarn and work to end. Working both sides at the same time, dec 1 st at both neck edges on next and ev row 16 (16, 16, 16, 16, 16) times. Cast off last st.

FRONT

Work as for back to ***.
Then *at the same time* when work measures 26.5 (26.5, 27, 27, 27, 27)in/ 67.25 (67.25, 68.5, 68.5, 68.5, 68.5)cm from c.o.e., ending on WS row, **shape neckline:**
Next row (RS) Work as set to centre 16 (16, 18, 18, 20, 20) sts, place these sts on holder, join a second ball of yarn and work to end. Working both sides at the same time, dec 1 st at both neck edges (whilst cont with armhole shaping) on next and ev row 4 (4, 8, 8, 6, 6) times, then ev alt row 12 (12, 10, 10, 13, 13) times. Cast off last st.

FINISHING

Armbands

With RS facing, using smaller ndles, starting at armhole edge, pick up and k5 (5, 5, 6, 6, 7) sts along straight edge of armhole, k24 (24, 26, 26, 30, 30) to top of armhole edge, break the yarn, then using smooth waste yarn cast on 10 (10, 10, 10, 12, 12) sts by provisional crochet method. Then turn the work and rejoin yarn and with RS facing cont around armhole - pick up and k24 (24, 26, 26, 30, 30) down other side of armhole and k5 (5, 5, 6, 6, 7) sts along straight edge – 68 (68, 72, 74, 84, 86) sts. Work 0.75in/2cm of openwork stitch and then work picot point cast-off.

Neckband

With RS facing, using circular ndle, starting at top back neck edge, place 10 (10, 10, 10, 12, 12) live sts on ndle from provisional cast-on (pull out the crochet and place the live sts on ndle), pick up and k20 (20, 20, 20, 22, 22) sts down sloping edge of front neck, k16 (16, 18, 18, 20, 20) sts from holder at centre front, k20 (20, 20, 20, 22, 22) sts up other side of front neck, place 10 (10, 10, 10, 12, 12) live sts on ndle from other provisional cast-on, pick up and k12 sts down back neck edge, 16 (16, 18,

18, 20, 20) sts from holder at centre back,
and k12 sts up other side back neck edge –
116 (116, 120, 120, 132, 132) sts.
Working in the round, cont as foll:
Row 1 *yrn, p2tog; rep from * to end
Row 2 *p2tog, yrn; rep from * to end
When 0.75in/2cm have been worked, cast
off using picot point cast-off.

Join side seams down to 1in/2.5cm below
top of slit.

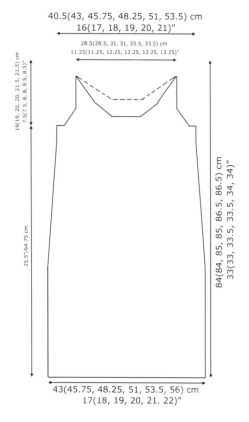

40.5(43, 45.75, 48.25, 51, 53.5) cm
16(17, 18, 19, 20, 21)"

28.5(28.5, 31, 31, 33.5, 33.5) cm
11.25(11.25, 12.25, 12.25, 13.25, 13.25)"

19(19, 20, 20, 21.5, 21.5) cm
7.5(7.5, 8, 8, 8.5, 8.5)"

25.5"/64.75 cm

84(84, 85, 85, 86.5, 86.5) cm
33(33, 33.5, 33.5, 34, 34)"

43(45.75, 48.25, 51, 53.5, 56) cm
17(18, 19, 20, 21. 22)"

STITCHES
Stocking stitch
Provisional cast-on
See Information page 76
Openwork stitch
All rows *yrn, p2tog; rep
from * to end
Picot point cast-off
Cast off 2 sts, *slip rem st on
RH ndle onto LH ndle, cast on
1 st, cast off 3 sts; repeat
from * to end and fasten off
rem st.

Playa

SIZE
15in/38cm wide x 13in/33cm high

MATERIALS
Araucania Nature Cotton:
4 skeins PT707/KFI-41
One pair 5.5mm (US 9)
needles *or size to obtain tension*
One 4.5mm crochet hook
(US 7)

TENSION
16 sts and 20 rows =
4in/10cms over chart pattern

STITCHES
See chart for main piece

Cable Pattern
(for top of bag)
Row 1(RS)
p2, k5, p1, k5, p1, k14
Row 2
p14, k1, p5, k1, p5, k2
Row 3
p2, c5f, p1, c5b, p1, k14
Rows 4, 6, 8 & 10
as row 2
Rows 5, 7 & 9
as row 1
Rep these 10 rows to end.

TO MAKE BAG

Main piece (back and front worked in one piece)

Cast on 61 sts and work 1 row as foll:

Row 1 sl 1, p1, k1, p1, k1, *(p1, k1) 3 times, p1, k2, (p1, k1) 4 times, rep from *3 times, p1, k1, p1, k1, k1 tbl

Then refer to chart and starting on WS row, work 96 rows, centring the chart as foll:

Chart row 1(WS) sl 1, k1, p1, k1, p1, work chart 3 times across row, k1, p1, k1, p1, k1 tbl

Cont as set keeping selvedge sts and 1 st of double moss st correct at each side of chart sts. When 96 rows are done, work 1 more row as row 1. Cast off in moss st.

Cabled top

Mark position of slits for handles on cast-on (front) and cast-off (back) edges of main piece. Slits should be 5in/12.5cm long and 5/12.5cm in from outer edges. Cast on 28 sts and work in cable patt until strip will travel around top and bottom edges of bag, ending on row 10.

At the same time, guided by your markers, make slits for front and back as foll:

Next row (RS) Work 8 sts, join a second ball of yarn and work 12 sts, join a third ball of yarn and work to end. Working all three pieces at the same time, work 5in/12.5cm slit ending on WS row, then work across all 28 sts on foll row.

FINISHING

Press to size on inside. Using a small neat backstitch on edge of work, join right seam, then sew cabled top to bag along cast-on and cast-off edges of main piece.

Join left side seam, including cabled top. Turn facing at top of bag to inside along foldline and slipstitch in place. With RS facing work 1 row of double crochet around slits to join two thicknesses of handles.

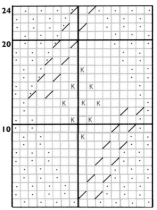

17 sts

NB CHART STARTS ON WS ROW

☐ knit on RS rows, purl on WS rows

· purl on RS rows, knit on WS rows

╱╱╱ slip 1 st onto cable needle and hold at back, k2, then k1 from cn

╱╱╱ slip 1 st onto cn and hold at back, k2, then p1 from cn

K work KNOT on this st - *k1, p1, k1, p1, k1 to make five sts from one, then pass 2nd, 3rd, 4th and 5th sts, one at a time, over first st, then slip first st onto LH needle and knit into back of it

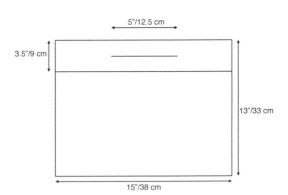

Lagoon

BACK

Using smaller ndles and A, cast on 94 (98, 102, 106, 114, 118) sts and work 1.25in/3cm in k2, p2 rib, ending on WS row, inc 0 (2, 2, 4, 2, 4) sts evenly across final row – 94 (100, 104, 110, 116, 122) sts. Change to larger ndles and cont in st st in striped patt above.

When work measures 19.5 (19.25, 19, 19.75, 19.5, 19.25)in/49.5 (48.75, 48.25, 50, 49.5, 48.75)cm, from c.o.e ending on WS row **shape armhole:**

Dec 1 st at both ends of next and every foll alt row 9 (10, 12, 14, 17, 18) times in all, keeping striped patt correct – 76 (80, 80, 82, 82, 86) sts. Cont as set until work measures 24.75 (24.75, 24.75, 25.75, 25.75, 25.75)in/63 (63, 63, 65.5, 65.5, 65.5)cm ending on WS row then **work neck:**

NB should end on completed *stripe 5* for XS, S & M, and after 1in/2.5cm of *stripe 6* for L, XL & XXL. For XS, S & M cont to end in A. For L, XL & XXL finish *stripe 6* then cont to end in A.

Next row (RS)   Work 22 sts, place centre 32 (36, 36, 38, 38, 42) sts on holder, join a second ball of yarn and work to end. Working both sides at the same time and cont to end in A, work 1 row, then dec 1 st at both neck edges on ev foll row 21 times. Cast off last st.

FRONT

Work as for back until work measures 23.25 (23.25, 23.25, 24.25, 24.25, 24.25)in/ 59 (59, 59, 61.5, 61.5, 61.5)cm ending on WS row. Then using A, change to smaller ndles and work 1.25in/3cm in k2, p2 rib, centring rib as foll:
k1, *p2, k2; rep from * to last 3 sts, p2, k1.

Cast off in rib.

LEFT SLEEVE

Using smaller ndles and C, cast on 50 (50, 50, 54, 54, 54) sts and work 1.25in/3 cm in k2, p2 rib, ending on WS row. Change to larger ndles and cont in st st in striped patt, working the remainder of *stripe 1* in A adjusting as follows so that stripes match at armholes:

Stripe 1   Work 1.25in/3cm in C in k2, p2 rib, work 3 (3, 3.25, 2, 1.75, 2)in/ 7.75 (7.75, 8.25, 5, 4.5, 5)cm in A in st st.

Work *stripe 2* in B, then cont with *stripes 5 & 6* and repeat these two to end.

At the same time inc after rib as follows:

XS   inc 1 st at both ends of 11th, then ev foll 12th row 7 times, then ev 10th row 3 times – 72sts

S   inc 1 st at both ends of 11th, then ev foll 12th row twice, then ev 10th row 9 times – 74sts

M   inc 1 st at both ends of 11th, then ev foll 10th row 9 times, then ev 8th row 3 times – 76sts

L   inc 1 st at both ends of 9th, then ev foll 10th row 7 times, then ev 8th row 5 times – 80sts

XL   inc 1 st at both ends of 9th, then ev foll 10th row 3 times, then ev 8th row 10 times – 82sts

XXL inc 1 st at both ends of 9th, then ev foll 8th row 10 times, then ev 6th row 5 times – 86sts

Cont in patt as set until work measures 20.25 (20, 20, 19.5, 19, 19)in/51.5 (50.75, 50.75, 49.5, 48.25, 48.25)cm and then shape **top of sleeve:**

Dec 1 st at both ends of next and every foll alt row 9 (10, 12, 14, 17, 18) times in all,

keeping striped patt correct. Cast off rem 54 (54, 52, 52, 48, 50) sts loosely.

RIGHT SLEEVE

Work as for left sleeve, but work *stripe 1* entirely in A:

Stripe 1 Work 1.25in/3cm in A in k2, p2 rib, work 3 (3, 3.25, 2, 1.75, 2)in/7.75 (7.75, 8.25, 5, 4.5, 5)cm in A in st st.

Work *stripe 2* in B, then cont with *stripes 5 & 6* and repeat these two to end, but work fourth contrasting stripe in C (worked in B for the first three contrasting stripes).

FINISHING
Back neck edge

Using smaller ndles and A, with RS facing and starting at right armhole edge, pick up and k18 (18, 18, 19, 19, 19) sts down sloping edge 32 (36, 36, 38, 38, 42) sts

from holder at centre back and pick up and k18 (18, 18, 19, 19, 19) sts up other sloping edge as before – 68 (72, 72, 76, 76, 80) sts. Work 1.25in/3cm in k2, p2 rib, centring the rib as foll:

k1, *p2, k2; rep from * to last 3 sts, p2, k1.
Cast off in rib.

Find centre of top of sleeve and mark. Sew back to sleeves so that the extra 3in/7.5cm of the triangles go down the front, 3in/7.5cm beyond the centre sleeve mark. Sew front to sleeves so that top of front ends on inside of triangles, 1.5in/3.75cm below centre sleeve mark, with triangles ending just below the front rib.

Do not sew sloping edge of triangle. Insert sleeves, placing any fullness evenly over whole sleeve cap. Join side and sleeve seams in one line, leaving 1in/2.5cm gap above sleeve rib for thumbs.

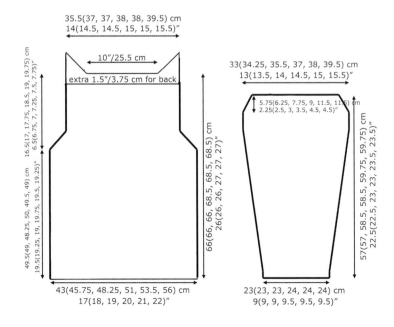

35.5(37, 37, 38, 38, 39.5) cm
14(14.5, 14.5, 15, 15, 15.5)"

10"/25.5 cm

extra 1.5"/3.75 cm for back

16.5(17, 17.75, 18.5, 19, 19.75)"
6.5(6.75, 7, 7.25, 7.5, 7.75)"

49.5(49, 48.25, 50, 49.5, 49) cm
19.5(19.25, 19, 19.75, 19.5, 19.25)"

66(66, 66, 68.5, 68.5, 68.5) cm
26(26, 26, 27, 27, 27)"

43(45.75, 48.25, 51, 53.5, 56) cm
17(18, 19, 20, 21, 22)"

33(34.25, 35.5, 37, 38, 39.5) cm
13(13.5, 14, 14.5, 15, 15.5)"

5.75(6.25, 7.75, 9, 11.5, 11.5) cm
2.25(2.5, 3, 3.5, 4.5, 4.5)"

57(57, 58.5, 58.5, 59.75, 59.75) cm
22.5(22.5, 23, 23, 23.5, 23.5)"

23(23, 23, 24, 24, 24) cm
9(9, 9, 9.5, 9.5, 9.5)"

CASA
PATTERNS

Firefly

SIZES

XS	to fit bust 32in/81.25cm
S	to fit bust 34in/86.25cm
M	to fit bust 36in/91.5cm
L	to fit bust 38in/96.5cm
XL	to fit bust 40in/101.5cm
XXL	to fit bust 42in/106.5cm

See schematic for actual measurements.

MATERIALS

Araucania Pomaire:
5 (5, 5, 5, 6, 6) skeins
PT696/KFI-64
One pair each 4mm
(US 6) and 4.5mm (US 7)
needles *or size to obtain tension*
One circular 4mm (US 6)
Stitch holders and markers
8 x 17mm buttons

TENSION

18 sts and 34 rows =
4in/10cms over braided
openwork pattern.

STITCHES

Moss stitch
See Information page 76
Braided openwork
Multiple of 2 sts
Row 1 (WS) p
Row 2 (RS) k1, *sl 1, k1,
        psso, m1; rep
        from * to last st,
        k1
Row 3 p
Row 4 k1, *m1, k2tog;
        rep from * to
        last st, k1

BACK

Using smaller ndles, cast on 74 (78, 84, 88, 92, 98) sts and work 7 rows in moss stitch ending on a RS row. Change to larger ndles and cont in braided openwork patt to end. When work measures 9.5in/24cm from c.o.e ending on WS row and then **shape armhole:**

Cast off 4 (4, 4, 5, 5, 5) sts at beg of next 2 rows. Then dec 1 st at both ends of next and ev foll alt row 3 (4, 6, 6, 7, 10) times in all, keeping patt correct as set – 60 (62, 64, 66, 68, 68) sts. Cont in patt as set until work measures 16.5 (16.5, 17, 17, 17,5, 17.5)in/42 (42, 43, 43, 44.5, 44.5)cm from c.o.e. ending on WS row and then **shape shoulder and neck:**

Next row (RS) Work 20 (21, 21, 22, 22, 22) sts, place centre 20(20, 22, 22, 24, 24) sts on holder, join a second ball of yarn and work to end. Working both sides at the same time, dec1 st at both neck edges on next and foll alt row.

At the same time work and place 6 sts on holder at armhole edge on next row, (for left back neck it will be foll row), and 6 (6, 6, 7, 7, 7) sts on foll alt row. Cast off over all 18 (19, 19, 20, 20, 20) sts.

LEFT FRONT

Using smaller ndles, cast on 43 (45, 47, 49, 51, 55) sts and work 7 rows in moss st] ending on a RS row. Change to larger ndles and cont as foll:
Place 5 sts at beg of next row (centre front) on holder and cont on rem 38 (40, 42, 44, 46, 50) sts in braided openwork patt to end. When work measures 9.5in/24cm from c.o.e ending on WS row, shape **armhole:**

Cast off 4 (4, 4, 5, 5, 5) sts at beg of next row. Work 1 row. Then dec 1 st at beg of next and ev foll alt row 3 (4, 6, 6, 7, 10) times in all, keeping patt correct as set – 31 (32, 32, 33, 34, 35) sts. Cont in patt as set until work measures 14.5 (14.5, 15, 15, 15.5, 15.5)in/37 (37, 38, 38, 39.5, 39.5)cm from c.o.e. ending on WS row and then **shape neck:**

Work and place 6 (6, 6, 6, 7, 8) sts at beg of next row on holder, then dec 1 st at neck edge on next and ev foll alt row 7 times. Cont until work measures 16.5 (16.5, 17, 17, 17,5, 17.5)in/42 (42, 43, 43, 44.5, 44.5)cm from c.o.e. ending on WS row, then **shape shoulder:**

Work and place 6 sts on holder at armhole edge. Work 1 row.
Work and place 6 (6, 6, 7, 7, 7) sts on holder at armhole edge. Work 1 row.
Cast off over whole 18 (19, 19, 20, 20, 20) sts.

RIGHT FRONT

Work as for left front reversing all shapings and front band.

SLEEVES

Using smaller ndles, cast on 40 (40, 42, 44, 46, 46) sts and work 7 rows in moss st] ending on a RS row. Change to larger ndles and cont in braided openwork patt to end inc as foll keeping patt correct as set:

XS	Inc 1 st at both ends of 25th, then ev foll 26th row 4 times – 50 sts
S	Inc 1 st at both ends of 19th, then ev foll 22nd row 5 times – 52 sts
M	Inc 1 st at both ends of 13th, then ev foll 20th row 6 times – 56 sts
L	Inc 1 st at both ends of 15th, then ev

foll 16th row 7 times – 60 sts

XL Inc 1 st at both ends of 17th, then ev foll 16th row 7 times – 62 sts

XXL Inc 1 st at both ends of 15th, then ev foll 14th row 8 times – 64 sts

Cont as set until work measures 18 (18, 18.5, 18, 18.5, 18.5,)in/45.75 (45.75, 47, 45.75, 47, 47)cm from c.o.e ending on WS row and then **shape sleeve cap:**

Cast off 4 (4, 4, 5, 5, 5) sts at beg of next 2 rows. Then dec 1 st at both ends of next, then ev foll 4th row 9 (6, 3, 6, 6, 3) times, then ev 3rd row 1 (5, 9, 7, 7, 11) times – 20 (20, 22, 22, 24, 24) sts.

Cast off 2 sts at beg of next 4 rows. Cast off rem 12 (12, 14, 14, 16, 16) sts

FINISHING

Join shoulder seams.

Insert sleeves placing any fullness evenly over top of sleeve cap.

Join side and sleeve seams in one line.

Button band

Using smaller ndles, pick up 5 sts on holder at left front and cont in moss stitch until band fits snugly when stretched slightly. Attach the band as you knit to ensure it fits well, and leave live sts on holder at neck edge. Mark and attach position of 6 buttons: first one at top of welt, the sixth 1.75 (1.75, 1.75, 2, 2, 2)in/4.5 (4.5, 4.5, 5, 5)cm from top edge and the rest spaced evenly between.

Buttonhole band

As left band, inserting buttonholes on RS rows as follows (first buttonhole to start immediately on top of welt):

Work 3 sts, join a second ball of yarn and work to end. Working both sides at the same time, work 2 further rows, then work across all 5 sts on foll row.

Neckband

Using smaller ndles, with RS facing, starting at right centre front, cast on 7 sts, pick up and k5 sts from buttonhole band holder, 6 (6, 6, 6, 7, 8) sts from holder at right front neck edge, k13 sts up to shoulder, k2 sts at right back neck edge, 20 (20, 22, 22, 24, 24) sts from holder at centre back, k2 sts at left back neck edge, 13 sts down left neck edge, 6 (6, 6, 6, 7, 8) sts from holder at left front neck edge and k5 sts from button band holder – 79 (79, 81, 81, 85, 85)sts. Work 7 rows in moss stitch, working 7th and 8th buttonholes on 4th row (RS row) as foll:

Work 3 sts, cast off 2 sts, work 4 sts, cast off 2 sts, work to end of row. Cast on these sts when you come to them on foll row. Cast off in moss stitch after 7 rows.

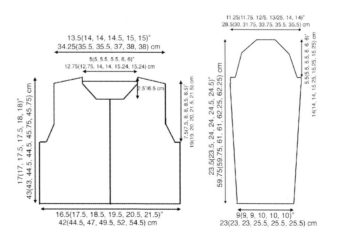

Ines

SIZES

XS   to fit bust 32in/81cm
S   to fit bust 34in/86cm
M   to fit bust 36in/91cm
L   to fit bust 38in/96cm
XL   to fit bust 40in/101cm
XXL to fit bust 42in/106cm
See schematic for actual
measurements

MATERIALS

Araucania Nature Cotton:
6 (6, 7, 7, 7, 8) skeins
PT552/KFI-21
One pair each 4.5mm (US 7)
and 5.5mm (US 9) *or size to
obtain tension*
One 30in/76cm long 5.5 (US 9)
circular needle
Stitch holders
3 x 30mm buttons

TENSION

14 sts and 20 rows =
4in/10cms over stocking
stitch

STITCHES

Garter stitch
Stocking stitch
See Information page 76

BACK

Peplum (worked in one piece for back and fronts)

Using circular ndle, but working back and forth in garter st, cast on 335 (347, 377, 389, 401, 416) sts. then cont as foll:

Rows 1-3   k

Row 4   k1, *k1, k2tog; rep from * to last 1st, k1 – 224 (232, 252, 260, 268, 278) sts

Rows 5-7   k

Row 8   k1 (2, 1, 1, 2, 1) *k1, k2tog; rep from * to last 1 (2, 2, 1, 2, 1) sts, k1 (2, 2, 1, 2, 1) – 150 (156, 169, 174, 180, 186) sts

Rows 9-11 k

Row 12   k1 (1, 2, 1, 1, 1) *k1, k2tog; rep from * to last 2 sts, k2 – 101 (105, 114, 117, 121, 125) sts

Rows 13-14 k

Change to larger straight ndles and cont in st st to end. Work and place first 25 (26, 28, 29, 30, 31) sts on holder for left front, work the foll 51 (53, 58, 59, 60, 62) sts, then work and place foll 25 (26, 28, 29, 30, 31) sts on holder for right front. Working on 51 (53, 58, 59, 60, 62) sts for back only, work 1 row then inc as follows:

XS (RS)   1st at both ends of 5th, then ev 8th row 3 times – 59 sts

S (RS)   1st at both ends of 5th, then ev 6th row 4 times – 63 sts

M (RS)   1st at both ends of 5th, then ev 8th row 3 times – 66 sts

L (RS)   1st at both ends of 5th, then ev 6th row 4 times – 69 sts

XL (RS)   1st at both ends of 5th, then ev 5th row 5 times – 72 sts

XXL (RS)   1st at both ends of 7th, then ev 4th row 6 times – 76 sts

Cont in st st as set until work measures 9.5in/24cm from c.o.e ending on WS row and then **shape armhole:**

Cast off 3 (3, 3, 4, 4, 4) sts at beg of next 2 rows. Then dec 1 st at both ends of next and every foll alt row 4 (5, 5, 5, 6, 7) times in all – 45 (47, 50, 51, 52, 54) sts.

Cont until work measures 16.25 (16.25, 16.75, 16.75, 17.25, 17.25)in/41.25 (41.25, 42.5, 42.5, 44, 44)cm from c.o.e. ending on WS row and then **shape shoulder and neck:**

Next row (RS) Work 16 (17, 18, 18, 18, 18) sts, place centre 13 (13,14, 15, 16, 18) sts on holder, join a second ball of yarn and work to end. Working both sides at the same time, dec 1 st at both neck edges on next and foll alt row.

At the same time work and place 4 (5, 5, 5, 5, 5) sts on holder at armhole edge on next row, (for left back neck it will be foll row), and 5 sts on foll alt row. Cast off over all 14 (15, 16, 16, 16, 16) sts.

LEFT FRONT

Using larger ndles and working in st st, with WS facing, work 25 (26, 28, 29, 30, 31) sts from holder for left front, Cont in st st to end, inc at outside edge (on right with RS facing) as foll:

XS (RS)   1st at beg of 5th, then ev 8th row 3 times – 29 sts

S (RS)   1st at beg of 5th, then ev 6th row 4 times – 31 sts

M (RS)   1st at beg of 5th, then ev 6th row 4 times – 33 sts

L (RS)   1st at beg of 5th, then ev 6th row 4 times – 34 sts

XL (RS)   1st at beg of 5th, then at outside edge ev 5th row 5 times – 36 sts

XL (RS) 1st at beg of 7th, then ev 4th row 6 times – 38 sts.

Cont in st st until work measures 9.5in/24 cm from c.o.e ending on WS row and then **shape armhole:**

Cast off 3 (3, 3, 4, 4, 4) sts at beg of next row. Work 1 row, then dec 1 st at armhole edge on next and ev foll alt row 4(5, 5, 5, 6, 7) times in all.

At the same time when work measures 9.5 (9.5, 10, 9.5, 10, 10)in/24 (24, 25.5, 24, 25.5, 25.5)cm from c.o.e ending on RS row, **shape neck:**

XS & S dec 1 st at beg of next, then ev foll 4th row 7 times – 14 (15) sts

M & L dec 1 st at beg of next, then ev foll 4th row 8 times – 16 (16) sts.

XL dec 1 st at beg of next, then at neck edge ev foll 3rd row 9 times – 16sts

XXL dec 1 st at beg of next, then at neck edge ev foll 3rd row 10 times – 16sts

Cont as set until work measures 16.25 (16.25, 16.75, 16.75, 17.25, 17.25)in/41.25 (41.25, 42.5, 42.5, 44, 44)cm from c.o.e. ending on WS row and then **shape shoulder:** Work and place 4 (5, 5, 5, 5, 5) sts on holder at armhole edge. Work 1 row. Work and place 5 sts on holder at armhole edge.

Cast off over all 14 (15, 16, 16, 16, 16) sts.

RIGHT FRONT

Using larger ndles and working in st st, with WS facing, work 25 (26, 28, 29, 30, 31) sts from holder for right front. Cont as for left front reversing all shapings.

SLEEVES

Peplum

Using circular ndle, but working back and forth in garter st, cast on 117 (123, 127, 135, 141, 141) sts. then cont as foll:

Rows 1-3 k

Row 4 *k1, k2tog; rep from * to last 0 (0, 1, 0, 0, 0) st, k0 (0, 1, 0, 0, 0) – 78 (82, 85, 90, 94, 94) sts

Rows 5-7 k

Row 8 *k1, k2tog; rep from * to last 0 (1, 1, 0, 1, 1) sts, k0 (1, 1, 0, 1,1) – 52 (55, 57, 60, 63, 63) sts

Rows 9-11 k

Row 12 *k1, k2tog; rep from * to last 1 (1, 0, 0, 0, 0) sts, k1 (1, 0, 0, 0, 0) – 35 (37, 38, 40, 42, 42) sts

Rows 13-14 k, inc 1 st at end of last row for sizes XS and S – 36 (38, 38, 40, 42, 42) sts

Change to larger straight needles and cont in st st to end, inc as foll:

XS & S inc 1 st at both ends of 23rd and foll 24th row – 40 (42) sts

M, L & XL inc 1 st at both ends of 17th, then ev foll 16th row twice – 44 (46, 48) sts

XXL inc 1 st at both ends of 15th, then ev foll 12th row 3 times – 50 sts

Cont in st st as set until work measures 13 (13, 13.5, 13, 13.5, 13.5)in/33 (33, 34.25, 33, 34.25, 34.25)cm from c.o.e ending on WS row and then **shape sleeve cap:**

Cast off 3 (3, 3, 4, 4, 4) sts at beg of next 2 rows. Then dec 1 st at both ends of next, then ev foll 3rd row 7 (5, 3, 5, 5, 3) times, then ev foll alt row 0 (3, 6, 4, 4, 7) times – 18 (18, 18, 18, 20, 20) sts.

Cast off 2 sts at beg of next 4 rows.

Cast off rem 10 (10, 10, 10, 12, 12) sts

Ines

FINISHING

Join shoulder seams.

Button band

Using smaller ndles cast on 6 sts and work in garter st until band will stretch from bottom of peplum to start of neck shaping. Band should fit snugly when stretched slightly. Sew it on to left front as you knit using a slipstitch, making sure there is not too much band for the sweater.

Buttonhole band

Mark position of three buttons on left band: 1st one at 2.75in/7cm from bottom, 3rd one 0.75in/2cm from the top and 2nd one spaced evenly between. Work as for button band, but attach to right front, adding 3 buttonholes on RS rows to correspond with buttons as foll: Work 2 st, cast off 2 sts, work 2 sts. Cast on these sts when you come to them on foll row.

Collar

Using smaller ndles, with WS facing and starting at **left** front neck edge, one stitch in along button band, pick up and k 30 (30, 30, 32, 32, 32 sts to shoulder seam, 2 sts down left back neck edge, 13 (13,14, 15, 16, 18) sts from holder at centre back, 2 sts up right back neck edge and 30 (30, 30, 32, 32, 32 sts down right front neck edge, finishing 1st in along cast-off edge of buttonhole band – 77 (77, 78, 83, 84, 86) sts. Working in garter st to end, work 0.5in/1.25 cm on smaller ndles ending on a WS row, then work 1.5in/3.75 cm on larger ndles. Cast off loosely

Insert sleeves placing any fullness evenly over top of sleeve cap. Join side and sleeve seams in one line.

Attach buttons opposite buttonholes.

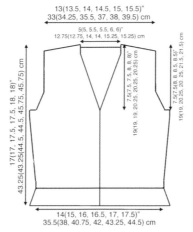

13(13.5, 14, 14.5, 15, 15.5)"
33(34.25, 35.5, 37, 38, 39.5) cm

5(5, 5.5, 5.5, 6, 6)"
12.75(12.75, 14, 14, 15.25, 15.25) cm

17(17, 17.5, 17.5, 18, 18)"
43.25(43.25(44.5, 44.5, 45.75, 45.75) cm

7.5(7.5, 7.5, 8, 8, 8)"
19(19, 19, 20.25, 20.25, 20.25) cm

7.5(7.5(8, 8.5, 8.5, 8.5)"
19(19, 20.25, 20, 21.5, 21.5) cm

14(15, 16, 16.5, 17, 17.5)"
35.5(38, 40.75, 42, 43.25, 44.5) cm

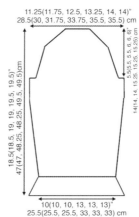

11.25(11.75, 12.5, 13.25, 14, 14)"
28.5(30, 31.75, 33.75, 35.5, 35.5) cm

5.5(5.5, 5.5, 6, 6, 6)"
15.25, 15.25, 15.25) cm

18.5(18.5, 19, 19, 19.5, 19.5)"
47(47, 48.25, 48.25, 49.5, 49.5)cm

14(14, 14, 15.25, 15.25, 15.25) cm

10(10, 10, 13, 13, 13)"
25.5(25.5, 25.5, 33, 33, 33) cm

Corbata

STITCHES

Garter stitch

see Information page 76

Scalloped stitch

Multiple of 18 + 1

Row 1	sl 1, yo, k7, sskpo, k7, yo, k1 tbl
Row 2	sl 1, k1 p15, k1, k1 tbl
Row 3	sl 1, k1, yo, k6, sskpo, k6, yo, k1, k1 tbl
Row 4	sl 1, k2, p13, k2, k1 tbl
Row 5	sl 1, k2, yo, k5, sskpo, k5, yo, k2, k1 tbl
Row 6	sl 1, k3, p11, k3, k1 tbl
Row 7	sl 1, k3, yo, k4, sskpo, k4, yo, k3, k1 tbl
Row 8	sl 1, k4, p9, k4, k1 tbl
Row 9	sl 1, k4, yo, k3, sskpo, k3, yo, k4, k1 tbl
Row 10	sl 1, k5, p7, k5, k1 tbl
Row 11	sl 1, k5, yo, k2, sskpo, k2, yo, k5, k1 tbl
Row 12	sl 1, k6, p5, k6, k1 tbl
Row 13	sl 1, k6, yo, k1, sskpo, k1, yo, k6, k1 tbl
Row 14	sl 1, k7, p3, k7, k1 tbl
Row 15	sl 1, k7, yo, sskpo, yo, k7, k1 tbl
Row 16	sl 1, knit to last st, k1 tbl

TO MAKE TIE

Cast on 19 sts and work 4 rows in garter st slipping the first st and knitting into the back of the last st. Refer to scalloped stitch and work the 16 rows.

Next row sl 1, k6, ssk, k1, k2tog, k6, k1 tbl Cont in garter st to end, keeping selvedge sts correct, dec 1 st (as above) at both sides of centre st ev 40th row 5 times – 7 sts. Cont on these 7 sts for 12in/30.5cm, then inc 1 st at both sides of centre st on next and foll 54th row as foll:

sl 1, k2, m1, k1, m1, k2, k1tbl

Cont on these 11 sts in garter st as set until work measures 50in/127 cm. Cast off.

FINISHING

Block to shape on WS.

SIZE

50in/127cm long x 2.75in/7cm at widest point

MATERIALS

Araucania Ulmo:
1 skein PT676/KFI-752
One pair 3.75mm (US 5) needles *or size to obtain tension*

TENSION

22 sts and 36 rows = 4in/10cms over garter stitch

2.75" 7 cm | 1.5" 3.75 cm

50"/127 cm

Desert Rose

SIZES

XS   to fit bust 32in/ 81.25cm
S   to fit bust 34in/ 86.2cm
M   to fit bust 36in/ 91.5cm
L   to fit bust 38in/ 96.5cm
XL   to fit bust 40in/101.5cm
XXL   to fit bust 42in/106.5cm
See schematic for actual
measurements

MATERIALS

Araucania Chacabuco:
6 (6, 7, 7, 8, 8) skeins
PT723/KFI-706
NB For more stitch definition,
substitute Araucania Nature
Cotton
One pair each 4.5mm
(US 7) and 5mm (US 8) or size to
obtain tension
Cable needle
Stitch holders
3 x 50mm buttons

TENSION

14 sts and 24 rows = 4in/10cms
over stocking stitch

BACK

Using larger ndles, cast on 64 (68, 72, 76, 80, 84) sts. Change to smaller ndles and work 6 rows in garter st. Change to larger ndles and cont in rev st st for 54 (54, 60, 60, 60, 60) rows, then dec as foll:

XS & S   1 st at both ends of 13th, then every 14th row twice – 58 (62) sts

M, L, XL, XXL 1 st at both ends of 15th, then every 16th row twice – 66 (70, 74, 78) sts

When 54 (54, 60, 60, 60, 60) rows are completed work 4 rows in garter st, then cont to end in st st. When work measures 12in/30.5cm from c.o.e. **shape armhole:**
Cast off 3 (3, 3, 4, 4, 4) sts at beg of next 2 rows. Dec 1 st at both ends of next, then every foll alt row 0 (0, 0, 0, 0, 3) times, then every foll 3rd row 1 (4, 7, 11, 10, 12) times then every foll 4th row 9 (7, 5, 2, 4, 1) times – 30 (32, 34, 34, 36, 36) sts. Cast off.

LEFT FRONT

Using larger ndles, cast on 51 (53, 55, 57, 59, 61) sts. Change to smaller ndles and work 6 rows in garter st, then change to larger ndles and cont as foll:

Row 1   p to last 24 sts, then work row 1 of cable pattern 1, k1, p11

Row 2   k11, p1, work row 2 of cable pattern 1, k to end.

The above 2 rows set the cable pattern 1. The last of these 2 rows represents row 2 (2,18,18,4,4) of cable patt 1. (See stitches section of pattern).
Cont in rev st st and cable patt 1 as set for 54 (54, 60, 60, 60, 60) rows, keeping the 11 sts of band facing (rev st st) and fold line st also correct.
At the same time dec as foll:

XS & S   1 st at beg of 13th, then every 14th row twice – 48 (50) sts

M, L, XL, XXL 1 st at beg of 15th, then every 16th row twice – 52 (54, 56, 58) sts

After 54 (54, 60, 60, 60, 60) rows are completed, work 4 rows as foll:

Row 1 (RS) k to last 24 sts, keep cable patt 1 correct (12 sts), k1, p11

Row 2   k11, p1, cable patt 1 – 12 sts, k to end.

Rep these 2 rows once. Then cont as foll to end:

Row 1 (RS) k to last 24 sts, keep cable patt 1 correct (12 sts), k1, p11

Row 2   k11, p1, cable patt 1 – 12 sts, p to end

Cont in st st and cable patt to end. When work measures 12in/30.5cm from c.o.e. ending on WS row and ending on row 14 (14,12,12,10,10) of cable pattern 1, then **shape armhole:**
Cast off 3 (3, 3, 4, 4, 4) sts at beg of next row. Work 1 row.
Dec 1 st at armhole edge of next, then every foll alt row 0 (0, 0, 0, 0, 4) times, then every foll 3rd row 0 (4, 6, 10, 8, 9) times then every foll 4th row 8 (5, 4, 1, 4, 1) times
At the same time when there are 38 (39, 40, 40, 41, 41) sts, ending on WS row, and row 6 of cable patt 1 has been completed begin neck shaping at same time, keeping raglan shaping correct as foll:

Next row   k6, cast off next 6 (7, 8, 8, 9, 9) sts, slip the st on right ndle and remaining sts onto a stitch holder, break yarn, turn. With WS of work facing rejoin yarn at neck edge. Dec 1st at neck edge on next 5 rows.

Next row   Fasten off

RIGHT FRONT

Work as for left front reversing all shapings and centre front band and cable crossing ie work c8b, so that cable slopes the other way. *At the same time* insert paired buttonholes in centre of the 4th and 5th cables (with parallel one in band facing) starting on row 9 (9, 11, 11, 11, 11) of cable patt 1 (RS row) and finishing on row 16 (16, 18, 18, 18, 18) as foll:

Working in patt as set, work 6 sts, turn and work a further 7 rows on these sts in patt. Leave these sts on holder, rejoin yarn and work 12 sts in patt as set, turn and work a further 7 rows on these 12 sts in patt. Leave on holder. Rejoin yarn to rem sts and work 8 rows in patt as set.
Work across all sts on foll row.

SLEEVES

Using larger ndles, cast on 50 (52, 54, 54, 58, 58) sts. Change to smaller ndles and work 4 rows garter st. Change to larger ndles and work 36 rows in cable patt 2, centring patt as foll:

RS rows   Rev st st – 1 (2, 3, 3, 1, 1) sts, rep cable patt 6 (6, 6, 6, 7, 7) times across row, rev st st – 1 (2, 3, 3, 1, 1) sts – 50 (52, 54, 54, 58, 58) sts.

Work a further 4 rows in garter st, then change to larger ndles and cont in st st to end, working first row as foll:

Next row (RS)

XS   k2, *k2tog, k2; rep from * to last 4 sts, k2tog, k2 – 38 sts

S   k3, *k2tog, k2; rep from * to last 5 sts, k2tog, k3 – 40 sts

M & L   k4, *k2tog, k3; rep from * to end – 44 sts

XL & XXL k6, *k2tog, k3; rep from * to last 7 sts, k2tog, k5 – 48 sts

Cont straight until work measures 12 (12, 12, 12.5, 12.5, 12.5)in /30.5 (30.5, 30.5, 31.75, 31.75, 31.75)cm from c.o.e ending on WS row, then **shape sleeve cap:**

Cast off 3 (3, 3, 4, 4, 4) sts at beg of next 2 rows. Then dec as foll:

Dec 1 st at both ends of next, then every alt row 1 (3, 6, 4, 6, 6) times, then every 3rd row 9 (8, 7, 8, 8, 8) times – 10 sts

Shape top of sleeve, starting on RS row for right sleeve and WS row for left sleeve. Cast off 2 sts at beg of next and foll alt row. Cast off 3 sts at beg of next and foll alt row.

FINISHING

Insert sleeves, joining the higher top sleeve edge to top back neck edge and lower top sleeve edge to top of fronts. Join side and sleeve seams in one line.

STITCHES

Garter stitch

Stocking stitch

Reverse stocking stitch

See Information page 76

Cable pattern 1

(for sizes XL, XXL)

Row 1   p2, k8, p2
Row 2   k2, p8, k2
Row 3   p2, k8, p2
Row 4   k2, p8, k2
Row 5   p2, c8f, p2
Row 6   k2, p8, k2
Rows 7, 9, 11, 13, 15, 17, 19   p2, k8, p2
Rows 8, 10, 12, 14, 16, 18, 20   k2, p8, k2

Rep these 20 rows to end

Cable pattern 1

(for sizes XS, S, M, L)

As above but finish on row 18 and rep these 18 rows

Cable pattern 1 (for collar)

As above but finish on row 16

Cable pattern 2 (all sizes)

Row 1   p2, k4, p2
Row 2   k2, p4, k2
Row 3   p2, c4f, p2
Rows 4, 6, 8   as row 2
Rows 5, 7   as row 1

Desert Rose

Collar

Using smaller ndles, with RS facing, starting at right centre front edge, pick up and work 24 sts from holder at centre front, then pick up and k15 (16, 17, 17, 18, 18) sts up sloping right neck edge and right sleeve, k24 (26, 28, 28, 30, 30) sts across centre back, k15 (16, 17, 17, 18, 18) sts along top of left sleeve and down sloping left neck edge and work 24 sts along horizontal left front neck edge – 102 (106, 110, 110, 114, 114) sts. K 1 row, keeping cable at centre fronts correct. Then work a further 16 rows in garter st, keeping cables and facing correct at centre front.

At the same time insert buttonhole in centre of the collar cable using buttonhole insertion process as before starting on the 10th row of collar cable pattern (NB not the 10th row of the 16 rows).

Next row (RS)   cast off purlwise 24 sts, p to last 24 sts, work in patt.
Next row (WS) cast off knitwise 24 sts, p to end

Cont in st st on rem 54 (58, 62, 62, 66, 66) sts until work measures 3in/7.5cm from fold line and then cast off loosely, on larger ndles if necessary.

Turn collar back onto inside and slipstitch in place around neck edge. Turn back bands along knit st fold line and slipstitch into place on inside along vertical and horizontal edges. Sew two layers of buttonholes together. Attach three buttons to left front band to correspond with buttonholes.

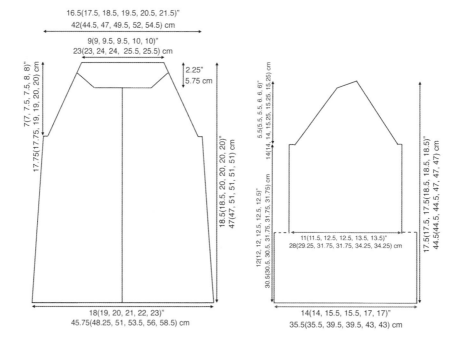

Pintor

BACK

Using smaller ndles, cast on 78 (82, 86, 90, 94, 98) sts and work 1.5in/4cm in k2, p2 rib, ending on WS row. Change to larger ndles and cont in st st. When work measures 17.5 (18, 18, 18.5, 18.5,18.5)in/44.5 (45.75, 45.75, 47, 47, 47)cm from c.o.e ending on WS row **shape armhole:**
Dec 1 st at both ends of next and every foll alt row 8 (9, 10, 11, 12, 13) times in all – 62 (64, 66, 68, 70, 72) sts. Cont as set until work measures 24 (24.5, 25, 25.5, 26, 26)in/61 (62.25, 63.5, 64.75, 66, 66)cm ending on WS row then **work neck:**
Next row (RS) Work 20 sts, place centre 22 (24, 26, 28, 30, 32) sts on holder, join a second ball of yarn and work to end.
Working both sides at the same time, work 1 row, then dec 1 st at both neck edges on ev foll row 19 times. Cast off last st.

FRONT

Work as for back until work measures 22 (22.5, 23, 23.5, 24, 24)in/56 (57, 58.5, 59.75, 61, 61)cm ending on WS row. Change to smaller ndles and work 2in/5cm in k2, p2 rib. *NB For S, L and XXL centre rib by working k3 instead of k2 at beg and end of row.* Cast off in rib.

SLEEVES

Using smaller ndles, cast on 38 (38, 38, 42, 42, 42) sts and work 1.5in/4cm in k2, p2 rib, ending on WS row. Change to larger ndles and cont in st st to end, inc 1 st at both ends of next, then ev foll 6th row 7 (8, 14, 8, 14, 14) times, then ev foll 8th row 5 (4, 0, 4, 0, 0) times – 64 (64, 68, 68, 72, 72) sts. Cont as set until work measures 20.25 (20, 20.5, 20, 20.5, 20.25)in/51.5 (51, 52, 51, 52, 51.5)cm and then shape **top of sleeve:**
Dec 1 st at both ends of next and every foll alt row 8 (9, 10, 11, 12, 13) times in all. Cast off rem 48 (46, 48, 46, 48, 46) sts loosely.

FINISHING

Back neck edge

Using smaller ndles with RS facing and starting at right armhole edge, pick up and k16 sts down sloping edge 22 (24, 26, 28, 30, 32) sts from holder at centre back and pick up and k16 sts up other sloping edge as before – 54 (56, 58, 60, 62, 64) sts. Work 2in/5cm in k2, p2 rib. *NB For S, L and XXL centre rib by working k3 instead of k2 at beg and end of row.* Cast off in rib.
Find centre of top of sleeve and mark. Sew back to sleeves so that the extra 4in/10 cm of the triangles goes down the front, 4in/10cm beyond the centre sleeve mark. Sew front to sleeves so that top of front ends on inside of triangles, 2in/5cm below centre sleeve mark. Do not sew sloping edge of triangle.
Join side and sleeve seams in one line.

SIZES

XS to fit chest 38in/96cm
S to fit chest 40in/101cm
M to fit chest 42in/106cm
L to fit chest 44in/111cm
XL to fit chest 46in/116cm
XXL to fit chest 48in/122cm
See schematic for actual measurements

MATERIALS

Araucania Patagonia:
9 (10, 10, 11, 11, 12) skeins
PT596/KFI-222
One pair each 5mm (US 8) and 5.5mm (US 9) needles
or size to obtain tension
Stitch holders

TENSION

15 sts and 20 rows =
4in/10cms over stocking stitch

STITCHES

K2, p2 rib
Stocking stitch
See Information page 76

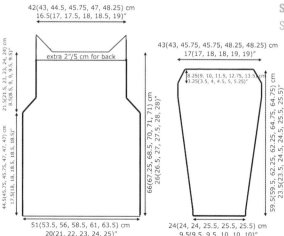

42(43, 44.5, 45.75, 47, 48.25) cm
16.5(17, 17.5, 18, 18.5, 19)"

extra 2"/5 cm for back

21.5(21.5, 23, 23, 24, 24) cm
8.5(8.5, 9, 9, 9.5, 9.5)"

44.5(45.75, 45.75, 47, 47, 47)cm
17.5(18, 18, 18.5, 18.5, 18.5)"

66(67.25, 68.5, 70, 71, 71) cm
26(26.5, 27, 27.5, 28, 28)"

51(53.5, 56, 58.5, 61, 63.5) cm
20(21, 22, 23, 24, 25)"

43(43, 45.75, 45.75, 48.25, 48.25) cm
17(17, 18, 18, 19, 19)"

8.25(9, 10, 11.5, 12.75, 13.5)cm
3.25(3.5, 4, 4.5, 5, 5.25)"

59.5(59.5, 62.25, 62.25, 64.75, 64.75) cm
23.5(23.5, 24.5, 24.5, 25.5, 25.5)"

24(24, 24, 25.5, 25.5, 25.5) cm
9.5(9.5, 9.5, 10, 10, 10)"

Cruz

S   32in wide x 7.5in
high/81.25cm x 19cm

M   35in wide x 11in
high/91.5cm x 28cm

L   40in wide x 14in
high/102cm x 35.5cm

MATERIALS

Araucania Pomaire:
1 (2, 2) skeins PT699/KFI-67 or
PT696/KFI-64 24in/61cm long
5mm
(US 8) circular needle *or size
to obtain tension*
Stitch marker

TENSION

16 sts and 10 rows =
4in/10cms over ripple stitch
pattern when blocked

TO MAKE SCARF

Cast on 130 (140, 160) sts, *loosely*.

Round 1   Ensuring sts are not twisted (very important), pick up and k1 st below the first cast-on st, along the lower edge of the cast-on row (ie k in the thread below the first cast-on st while leaving the first cast-on st on the ndle). This closes the circle. Continue around similarly, picking up one st below each of the original cast-on stitches, while leaving the cast-on stitches on their ndle – 260 (280, 320) sts. (NB The circular ndle will begin to coil up within itself during this round, but as the knitting progresses it will get easier.)

Round 2   Place a marker on the right ndle. Make sure the work is not twisted. Knit the first st in the normal way. Continue to k around until reached the marker.

Round 3   sl marker, p around

Round 4   sl marker, k around

Round 5   sl marker, p around

Round 6   sl marker, *k1, (yo) twice, k1, (yo) 3 times, k1, (yo) 4 times, k1, (yo) 3 times, k1, (yo) twice, k5; rep from * around

Round 7   sl marker, p around, dropping all yo's off ndle

Round 8   sl marker, k around

Round 9   sl marker, p around

Round 10   sl marker, *k6, (yo) twice, k1, (yo) 3 times, k1, (yo) 4 times, k1, (yo) 3 times, k1, (yo) twice, rep from * around

Round 11   sl marker, p around, dropping all yo's off ndle

S   work rounds 4-7, then rounds 2-5, then cast off knitwise – 19 rows in all

M   work rounds 4-11, then rounds 4-7, then rounds 2-5, then cast off knitwise – 27 rows in all

L   work rounds 4-11 twice more, then work rounds 4-7, then work rounds 2-5 once, then cast off knitwise – 35 rows in all.

FINISHING

Weave in ends along side edges.
Press to size.

16(17.5, 20)"
81(92, 102) cm

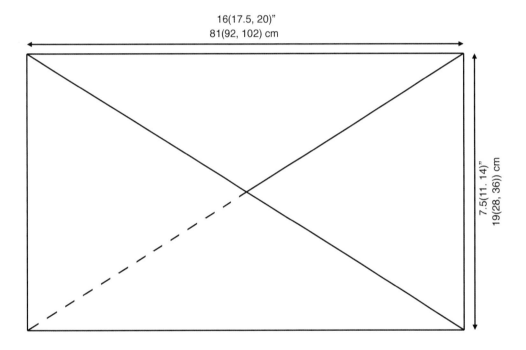

7.5(11. 14)"
19(28, 36)) cm

MONTANA
PATTERNS

Lava

SIZES

XS   to fit bust 32in/81cm
S   to fit bust 34in/86cm
M   to fit bust 36in/91cm
L   to fit bust 38in/96cm
XL   to fit bust 40in/101cm
XXL to fit bust 42in/106 cm
See schematic for actual
measurements

MATERIALS

Araucania Ulmo:
5 (6, 6, 6, 7, 7) skeins
PT676/KFI-752
One pair each 3.25mm (US 3)
and 4mm (US 6) needles *or
size to obtain tension*
Stitch holders
Large crochet hook
2 open-ended zips: for front
20.5 (20.5, 21, 21.5, 21.5)in/
52(52, 53.5, 54.5, 54.5)cm; for
hood top 9 (9, 9.5, 10, 10.5)in/
22.75 (23, 24, 25.5, 26.5)cm

TENSION

16 sts and 26 rows =
4in/10cms over lace pattern

STITCHES

Garter stitch
See Information page 76
Lace pattern
Multiple of 2 sts
All rows *yrn, sl 1, k1, psso;
rep from * to end

BACK

Using smaller ndles, cast on 66 (70, 74, 78, 82, 86) sts.

Work 6 rows in garter st, then change to larger ndles and cont in lace patt to end. When work measures 2 (2, 2, 1.5, 1.5, 1.5in/5 (5, 5, 4, 4, 4)cm from c.o.e ending on WS row, dec as foll:

XS, S   1 st at both ends of next, then ev foll 6th row 5 times, keeping lace patt correct – 54 (58) sts

M   1 st at both ends of next, then ev foll 7th row 5 times, keeping lace patt correct – 62 sts

L, XL & XXL 1 st at both ends of next, then ev foll 6th row 7 times, keeping lace patt correct – 62 (66, 70) sts.

Cont in patt as set for 10 rows, then inc as foll:

XS, S & M 1 st at both ends of next, then ev foll 6th row 5 times – 66 (70, 74) sts

L, XL & XXL 1 st at both ends of next, then ev foll 4th row 7 times – 78 (82, 86) sts

Cont in patt as set until work measures 15.5 (15.5, 15.5, 16, 15.5, 16)in /39.5 (39.5, 39.5, 40.5, 39.5, 40.5)cm from c.o.e. ending on a WS row, then **shape armhole:**

Cast off 3 (3, 3, 4, 4, 4) sts at beg of next 2 rows. Dec 1 st at both ends of next and ev foll alt row 4 (5, 6, 6, 7, 8) times in all – 52 (54, 56, 58, 60, 62) sts. Cont until work measures 22.25 (22.25, 22.75, 23.25, 23.25, 23.75)in/56.5 (56.5, 57.75, 59, 59, 60.5)cm from c.o.e. ending on WS row, then shape **shoulder and neck:**

Next row (RS) Work 16 (16, 17, 17, 18, 18) sts, place centre 20 (22, 22, 24, 24, 26) sts on holder, join a second ball of yarn

and work to end. Working both sides at the same time, dec 1 st at both neck edges on next and foll alt row.

At the same time work and place 4 (5, 5, 5, 5, 5) sts on holder at armhole edge on next row, (for left back neck it will be foll row), and 5 sts on foll alt row.

Cast off over all 14 (14, 15, 15, 16, 16) sts.

LEFT FRONT

Using smaller ndles, cast on 34 (36, 38, 40, 42, 44) sts. Work 6 rows in garter st, then change to larger ndles and cont as foll to end:

Next row Work lace patt to last 2 sts, k2

Cont in this way in patt, keeping the 2 sts of garter st at centre front to end.

When work measures 2 (2, 2, 1.5, 1.5, 1.5)in/5 (5, 5, 4, 4, 4)cm from c.o.e. ending on WS row, dec as foll, keeping patt correct:

XS, S   1 st at beg of next, then ev foll 6th row 5 times – 28 (30) sts

M   1 st at beg of next, then at armhole edge ev foll 7th row 5 times – 32 sts

L, XL & XXL 1 st at beg of next, then ev foll 6th row 7 times – 32 (34, 36) sts.

Cont in patt as set for 10 rows, then inc as foll, keeping patt correct:

XS, S & M 1 st at beg of next, then at armhole edge on ev foll 6th row 5 times – 34 (36, 38) sts

L, XL & XXL 1 st at beg of next, then ev foll 4th row 7 times – 40 (42, 44) sts

At the same time when work measures 3in/7.5cm from c.o.e. ending on WS row, **work pocket:**

Work and place on holder 8 (10, 10, 10, 12, 12) sts. Rejoin yarn to rem sts and dec 1 st

at beg of 1st row, then at pocket edge every 6th row 5 times. Leave sts on holder. Return to 8 (10,10, 10, 12, 12) sts on holder, rejoin yarn and cast on 20 (20,20, 22, 22, 22) sts. Keeping shaping correct at outside edge, work 31 rows in patt as set, casting off 14 (14, 14, 16, 16, 16) sts at beg of final row. Work across all sts and cont with shaping as above.

Cont as set until work measures 15.5 (15.5, 15.5, 16, 15.5, 16)in/39.5 (39.5, 39.5, 40.5, 39.5, 40.5)cm from c.o.e. ending on a WS row, then **shape armhole:**
Cast off 3 (3, 3, 4, 4, 4) sts at beg of next row. Work 1 row, then dec 1 st at beg of next and ev foll alt row 4 (5, 6, 6, 7, 8) times in all – 27 (28, 29, 30, 31, 32) sts.
Cont until work measures 20.5 (20.5, 21, 21.5, 21.5, 22) in/ 52 (52, 53.5, 54.5, 54.5, 56)cm from c.o.e. ending on RS row, then **shape neck:**
Work and place 7 (8, 8, 9, 9, 10) sts on holder, then dec 1 st at beg of next and ev foll alt row 6 times in all – 14 (14, 15, 15, 16, 16) sts.
Cont until work measures 22.25 (22.25, 22.75, 23.25, 23.25, 23.75)in/56.5 (56.5, 57.75, 59, 59, 60.5)cm from c.o.e. ending on WS row, then **work shoulder:**
Work and place 4 (5, 5, 5, 5, 5) sts on holder at armhole edge on next row, and 5 sts on foll alt row. Cast off over all 14 (14, 15, 15, 16, 16) sts.

RIGHT FRONT

Work as for left front reversing all shapings and pockets and centre front band.

SLEEVES

Using smaller ndles, cast on 40 (40, 42, 42, 44, 44) sts. Work 6 rows in garter st, then change to larger ndles and cont in lace pattern to end, inc as foll, keeping patt correct as set:

XS	1 st at both ends of 39th, then foll 38th row – 44 sts
S	1 st at both ends of 29th, then ev foll 28th row twice – 46 sts
M	1 st at both ends of 23rd, then ev foll 24th row 3 times – 50 sts
L & XL	1 st at both ends of 17th, then ev foll 16th row 5 times – 54 (56) sts
XXL	1 st at both ends of 15th, then ev foll 16th row 6 times – 58 sts

Cont as set until work measures 18 (18, 18.25, 18.25, 18.5, 18.5)in /45.75 (45.75, 46.5, 46.5 47, 47)cm from c.o.e. ending on WS row and then **shape sleeve cap:**
Cast off 3 (3, 3, 4, 4, 4) sts at beg of next 2 rows. Then, keeping patt correct as set, dec 1 st at both ends of next, then ev 3rd row 9 times, then ev alt row 0 (0, 1, 1, 2, 2) times – 18 (20, 22, 24, 24, 26) sts. Cast off 2 sts at beg of next 4 rows.
Cast off rem 10 (12, 14, 16, 16,18) sts.

FINISHING

Join shoulder seams.

Hood

Using larger ndles, with RS facing and starting at right centre front, pick up and k7 (8, 8, 9, 9, 10) sts from holder at centre front, k9 sts up sloping edge of neck, k4 sts up straight side of neck, k2 sts down back neck, k20 (22, 22, 24, 24, 26) sts from holder at centre back, k2 sts up other side back neck, k4 sts down left front neck edge, k9 sts down sloping edge of neck

Lava

and k7 (8, 8, 9, 9, 10) sts from holder at left centre front – 64 (68, 68, 72, 72, 76) sts.

Work 12.5in/ 31.75cm as foll:

All rows   k2, *yrn, sl 1, k1, psso; rep from * to last 2 sts, k2

Work 4 rows in garter st and then cast off as foll:

k1, *m1, cast off 1 st, k1, cast off 1 st; rep from * to end.

Pocket edgings

Using smaller ndles, with RS facing, pick up and k24 sts along sloping edge of pockets. Knit 5 rows and then cast off knitwise. Slipstitch side edges at top and bottom to sweater. Sew pocket linings in place on inside using invisible slipstitch.

Insert sleeves placing any fullness evenly over top of sleeve cap. Join side and sleeve seams in one line, leaving thumb-sized gap 1in/2.5cm from cuff edge. Sew open-ended zips into front and along top edge of hood, zipper to be at centre back of hood when closed.

Position the zip 2 sts in from the edge to prevent the teeth from showing and sew in place with a backstitch.

Tassel

Measure out 10 x 18in/45cm pieces of yarn. Fold in two and thread folded end through zip fastener. Attach the tassel by pulling the threads through the loop formed. Trim to preferred length.

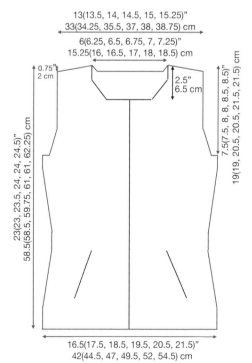

13(13.5, 14, 14.5, 15, 15.25)"
33(34.25, 35.5, 37, 38, 38.75) cm

6(6.25, 6.5, 6.75, 7, 7.25)"
15.25(16, 16.5, 17, 18, 18.5) cm

0.75"
2 cm

2.5"
6.5 cm

7.5(7.5, 8, 8, 8.5, 8.5)"
19(19, 20.5, 20.5, 21.5, 21.5) cm

23(23, 23.5, 24, 24, 24.5)"
58.5(58.5, 59.75, 61, 61, 62.25) cm

16.5(17.5, 18.5, 19.5, 20.5, 21.5)"
42(44.5, 47, 49.5, 52, 54.5) cm

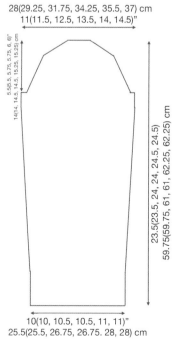

28(29.25, 31.75, 34.25, 35.5, 37) cm
11(11.5, 12.5, 13.5, 14, 14.5)"

5.5(5.5, 5.75, 5.75, 6, 6)"
14(14, 14.5, 14.5, 15.25, 15.25) cm

23.5(23.5, 24, 24, 24.5, 24.5)"
59.75(59.75, 61, 61, 62.25, 62.25) cm

10(10, 10.5, 10.5, 11, 11)"
25.5(25.5, 26.75, 26.75. 28, 28) cm

Bola

TO MAKE HAT

Using A, cast on 88 (96, 104) sts and spread evenly over three of the 4 dpns. Work in st st in the round for 2.5in/6.5cm.

Next round   *[k8 (9,10), k2tog], rep from * to last 8 sts, k8 – 80 (88, 96) sts.

Work a further 1in/2.5cm and then cont as foll:

Next round (S) *k11, k2tog, rep from * to last 2 sts, k2 – 74 sts

Next round (M) *k10, k2tog, rep from * to last 4 sts, k4 – 81 sts

Next round (L) *k11, k2tog, rep from * to last 5 sts, k5 – 89 sts

Cont in st st as set until work measures 9.5 (9.5,10)in/24(24, 25)cm from c.o.e., then **shape crown:**

Round 1   *k4, k2tog; repeat from * to last 2 (3, 5) sts, k2 (3, 5) – 62 (68, 75) sts

Round 2   k

Round 3   k3, k2tog; repeat from * to last 2(3, 0) sts, k2 (3, 0) – 50 (55, 60) sts

Round 4   k

Round 5   k2, k2tog; repeat from * to last 2(3, 0) sts, k2 (3, 0) – 38 (42, 45) sts

Round 6   k

Round 7   * k1, k2tog; repeat from * to last 2(0, 0) sts, k2 (0, 0) – 26 (28, 30) sts

Round 8   k

Round 9   *k2tog across row – 13 (14, 15) sts

Round 10   k

*Round 11**   k2tog across row – 7 (7, 8) sts

Round 12   k

Break off yarn, thread through remaining sts and secure firmly on inside.

FINISHING

Press to shape on inside.

Style 1   Using crochet hook and B used double, work chain to travel around hat plus extra 8in/20cm. Knot at each end and tie around hat above roll to finish at centre back.

Style 2   Using two 4mm needles and B, cast on 21 sts and work 3 rows in garter st. Pass all sts one at a time over first st, then fasten off. Turn cast-on edge into cast-off edge with one twist to form flower. Make enough to go round brim fitting snugly, as when hat is worn they will space out. Stitch in place above rolled brim.

SIZES

S   18in/46cm finished circumference

M   20in/51cm finished circumference

L   22in/56cm finished circumference

MATERIALS

Style 1 Araucania Patagonia: 2 (2, 2) skeins PT576/KFI-206 (A) 10yds/m Chacabuco PT723/KFI-706 (B)

Style 2 Araucania Pomaire: 2 (2, 2) PT699/KF-I67 (A) 10yds/m Pomaire PT635/KFI-108 (B)

Four 4mm (US 6) double pointed needles *or size to obtain tension*

One 6.5 mm crochet hook (US K/10.5)

TENSION

16 sts and 24 rows = 4in/10cms over stocking stitch

STITCHES

Stocking stitch (in the round) Knit every row

Rocco

BACK

Using smaller ndles and B, cast on 72 (76, 80, 82, 86, 90) sts.

Work 8 rows in garter st, then change to larger ndles and A and cont in st st to end. When work measures 16 (16, 16.5, 16.5, 17, 17)in/40.5 (40.5, 42, 42, 43.25, 43.25)cm from c.o.e. ending on a WS row, then **shape armhole:**

Cast off 4 (4, 4, 5, 5, 5) sts at beg of next 2 rows. Dec 1 st at both ends of next and following 2 (3, 4, 3, 4 ,5) alt rows – 58 (60, 62, 64, 66, 68) sts. Cont until work measures 25 (25, 26, 26, 27, 27)in/63.5 (63.5, 66, 66, 68.5, 68.5)cm from c.o.e. ending on WS row, then shape **shoulder and neck:**

Next row (RS) Work 20 (20, 21, 21, 22, 22) sts, place centre 18 (20, 20, 22, 22, 24) sts on holder, join a second ball of yarn and work to end. Working both sides at the same time, dec 1 st at both neck edges on next and following alt row.

At the same time work and place 6 sts on holder at armhole edge on next row, (for left back neck it will be following row), and 6 (6, 6, 6, 7, 7) sts on foll alt row. Cast off over all 18 (18, 19, 19, 20, 20) sts.

LEFT FRONT

Using smaller ndles and B, cast on 37 (39, 41, 42, 44, 46) sts. Work 8 rows in garter st, then change to larger ndles and A and cont as foll to end:

Next row k

Next row k3, purl to end

Cont in this way in st st, keeping the 3 sts of garter st at centre front to end. When work measures 3in/7.5cm from c.o.e. ending on WS row, **work pocket:**

With RS of work facing, work and place on holder 9 (9, 9, 11, 11, 11) sts. Rejoin yarn to rem sts and dec 1 st at pocket edge beg of 1st row, then dec 1 st at pocket edge every 5th row 6 times ending on a RS row. With WS of work facing, work 1 row, then place sts on holder. With WS of work facing, return to 9 (9, 9, 11, 11, 11) sts on holder, rejoin yarn and cast on 22 (22,22, 24, 24, 24) sts. Work 31 rows in patt as set, casting off 15 (15, 15, 17, 17, 17) sts at beg of final row (this will be a WS row). Work across all sts on following row.

Cont as set until work measures 16 (16, 16.5, 16.5, 17, 17)in/40.5 (40.5, 42, 42, 43.25, 43.25)cm from c.o.e. ending on a WS row, then **shape armhole:**

Cast off 4 (4, 4, 5, 5, 5) sts at beg of next row. Work 1 row, then dec 1 st at beg of the next row and foll 3 (4, 5, 4, 5, 6) alt rows – 29 (30, 31, 32, 33, 34) sts.

Cont until work measures 23 (23, 24, 24, 24.5, 24.5)in/58.5 (58.5, 61, 61, 62.25, 62.25)cm from c.o.e. ending on RS row, then **shape neck:**

Work and place 6 (7, 7, 7, 7, 8) sts on holder, then dec 1 st at beg of next and 4 (4, 4, 5, 5, 5) foll alt rows – 18 (18, 19, 19, 20, 20) sts.

Cont until work measures 25 (25, 26, 26, 27, 27)in/63.5 (63.5, 66, 66, 68.5, 68.5)cm from c.o.e. ending on WS row, then **work shoulder:**

With RS of work facing, work and place 6 sts on holder at armhole edge on next row, and 6 (6, 6, 6, 7, 7) sts on foll alt row. Cast off over all 18 (18, 19, 19, 20, 20) sts.

RIGHT FRONT

Work as for left front reversing all

shapings, pockets and centre front band.

SLEEVES

Using smaller ndles and B, cast on 38 (38, 40, 40, 42, 42) sts. Work 8 rows in garter st, then change to larger ndles and A and cont in st st to end, inc as foll:

XS 1 st at both ends of 15th, then ev foll 12th row 5 times – 50 sts.

S 1 st at both ends of 15th, then ev foll 10th row 6 times – 52 sts

M 1 st at both ends of 17th, then ev foll 10th row 6 times – 54 sts

L 1 st at both ends of 9th, then ev foll 10th row 7 times – 56 sts

XL 1 st at both ends of 9th, then ev foll 10th row 7 times – 58 sts

XXL 1 st at both ends of 15th, then ev foll 8th row 8 times – 60 sts

Cont as set until work measures 18 (18, 18.5, 18.5, 19, 19)in/45.75 (45.75, 47, 47, 48.25, 48.25)cm from c.o.e. ending on WS row and then **shape sleeve cap:**

Cast off 4 (4, 4, 5, 5, 5) sts at beg of next 2 rows. Then, keeping patt correct as set, dec 1 st at both ends of next, then ev 3rd row 3 (3, 5, 5, 7, 5) times, then ev alt row 8 (8, 6, 6, 4, 7) times – 18 (20, 22, 22, 24, 24) sts. Cast off 2 sts at beg of next 4 rows. Cast off rem 10 (12, 14, 14, 16, 16) sts.

FINISHING

Join shoulder seams.

Hood

Using larger ndles and A, cast on 3 sts, then with RS facing and starting at right centre front, pick up and k6 (7, 7, 7, 7, 8) sts from holder at centre front, k12 (12, 12, 12, 14, 14) sts up sloping edge of neck to shoulder, k3 sts down back neck, k18 (20, 20, 22, 22, 24) sts from holder at centre back, k3 sts up other side back neck, k12 (12, 12, 12, 14, 14) sts down sloping left front neck edge, and k6 (7, 7, 7, 7, 8) sts from holder at left centre front, then cast on 3 sts – 66 (70, 70, 72, 76, 80) sts. Work as foll:

Row 1 k6, p to last 6 sts, k6
Row 2 k

Repeat these 2 rows.
When hood measures 1in/2.5cm ending on WS row, work holes for cord:

K3, yo, k2 tog, k to last 5 sts, yo, k2 tog, k3.
Cont in patt as set until work measures 13.5 (13.5, 14, 14, 14.5, 14.5)in/34.25 (34.25, 35.5, 35.5, 37, 37)cm change to smaller ndles and B and work 0.5in/1.25cm in garter st and then cast off loosely.

Pocket edgings

Using smaller ndles and B, with RS facing, pick up and k20 sts along sloping edge of pockets. Knit 5 rows and then cast off knitwise. Slipstitch side edges at top and bottom to sweater. Sew pocket linings in place on inside using invisible slipstitch. Insert sleeves placing any fullness evenly over top of sleeve cap. Join side and sleeve seams in one line, leaving thumb-sized gap 1in/2.5cm from cuff edge. With RS facing, fold hood in half and join along top edge. Fold hem back and slipstitch into place to make tube for cord.

Make cord

Using crochet hook and B, make a chain long enough to pass around edge of hood, with 8in/20cm to spare at each side – approx 42 (42, 43, 43, 44, 44)in/107 (107, 110, 110, 112, 112)cm. Insert cord, then knot at each end.

Sew open-ended zip into front: position the zip 2 sts in from the edge to prevent the teeth from showing and sew in place with a backstitch.

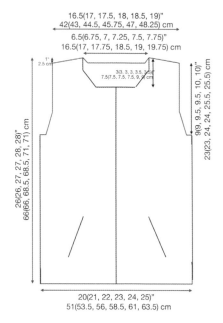

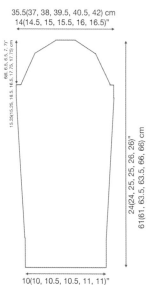

Caldera

SIZES

XS   to fit bust 32in/81cm
S   to fit bust 34in/86cm
M   to fit bust 36in/91cm
L   to fit bust 38in/96cm
XL   to fit bust 40in/101cm
XXL to fit bust 42in/106cm
See schematic for actual
measurements

MATERIALS

Araucania Ulmo:
3 (3, 3, 3, 3, 4) skeins
PT684/KFI-760
One pair each 3.25mm (US 3)
and 3.75mm (US 5) needles
or size to obtain tension

TENSION

22 sts and 32 rows =
4in/10cms over stocking
stitch.

STITCHES

1 x 1 rib
Stocking stitch
See Information page 76

BACK

Using smaller ndles, cast on 84 (89, 95, 100, 107, 112) sts.
Refer to Chart 1 and work 1.25in/3cm, centring chart as foll:

XS p1, k1, work chart 16 times across row, p1, k1

S   p1, k1, work chart 17 times across row, p1, k1

M   work chart 19 times across row

L   work chart 20 times across row

XL k1, work chart 21 times across row, p1

XXL k1, work chart 22 times across row, p1

Change to larger ndles and refer to Chart 2 and cont, centring chart as above, working sts at beg and end of repeats in st st. When work measures 8in/20.25cm from c.o.e. ending on row 4, change to smaller ndles and refer to Chart 1 and cont to end as before. When work measures 18.5 (18.5, 19, 19, 19.5, 19.5)in /47 (47, 48.25, 48.25, 49.5, 49.5)cm from c.o.e., ending on WS row, **shape shoulder and neck:**

Next row (RS)   Work 25 (27, 28, 30, 31, 33) sts, place centre 34 (35, 39, 40, 45, 46) sts on holder, join a second ball of yarn and work to end. Working both sides at the same time, dec 1 st at both neck edges on next and foll alt row.

At the same time work and place 7 (8, 8, 9, 9, 10) sts on holder at armhole edge on next row, (for left back neck it will be foll row), and 8 (8, 9, 9, 10, 10) sts on foll alt row. Cast off over all 23 (25, 26, 28, 29, 31) sts.

FRONT

Work as for back until work measures 12.5 (12.5, 13, 13, 13.5, 13.5)in/ 31.75 (31.75, 33, 33, 34.25, 34.25)cm from c.o.e. ending on a WS row, then **work straps:**

Next row
    Work 13 (15, 16, 18,19, 21) sts, place centre 58 (59, 63, 64, 69, 70) sts on holder, join a second ball of yarn and work to end. Working both sides at the same time, work 7 rows then, keeping patt correct, inc as foll:

Next row (left strap)
    Work to last 2 sts in patt, make 2 sts using backwards loop method (make backwards loop onto right ndle so that the yarn points towards you), p1, k1.

Next row (right strap)
    k1, p1, make 2 sts using backwards loop method (make a backwards loop onto right ndle, so that the working yarn points away from you), then work to end of row in patt.

Cont in Chart 1 patt, incorporating inc sts in patt, 2 rib sts in from neck edge ev foll 6th row until there are 23 (25, 26, 28, 29, 31) sts. Cont in patt as set until strap measures 6in/15.25cm then **shape shoulder:** Work and place 7 (8, 8, 9, 9, 10) sts on holder at armhole edge on next row, (for left back neck it will be foll row), and 8 (8, 9, 9, 10, 10) sts on foll alt row. Cast off over all 23 (25, 26, 28, 29, 31) sts.

FINISHING

Join right shoulder seam. Then using smaller ndles, with RS facing, pick up and k34 sts down left front neck edge, k55 (58, 63, 66, 71, 74) sts from holder at centre front, k34 sts up right front neck, k2 sts down right back neck, k33 (34, 39, 40, 45, 46) sts from holder at centre back and k2 sts up left back neck – 160 (164, 174, 178, 188, 192) sts. Knit 1 row and then cast off

knitwise. Join left shoulder seam. Join
side seams leaving 6.5 (6.5, 7, 7.
7.5.7.5)in/16.5 (16,5, 17.75, 17.75,19, 19)cm
for armhole. Insert ribbon through eyelets
and tie at centre front.

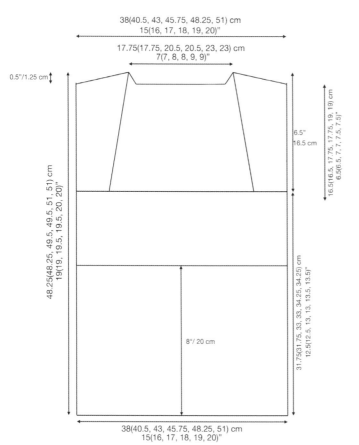

38(40.5, 43, 45.75, 48.25, 51) cm
15(16, 17, 18, 19, 20)"

17.75(17.75, 20.5, 20.5, 23, 23) cm
7(7, 8, 8, 9, 9)"

0.5"/1.25 cm

48.25(48.25, 49.5, 49.5, 51 , 51) cm
19(19, 19.5, 19.5, 20, 20)"

6.5"
16.5 cm

16.5(16.5, 17.75, 17.75, 19, 19) cm
6.5(6.5, 7, 7, 7.5, 7.5)"

31.75(31.75, 33, 33, 34.25, 34.25) cm
12.5(12.5, 13, 13, 13.5, 13.5)"

8"/ 20 cm

38(40.5, 43, 45.75, 48.25, 51) cm
15(16, 17, 18, 19, 20)"

Chart 1 · 5 sts   Chart 2 · 5 sts

knit on RS rows, purl on WS rows - st st

purl on RS rows, knit on WS rows - reverse st st

yarn over needle (to make a stitch)

ssk - slip, slip, knit - slip 2 sts knitwise, one at a time, then insert
LH needle into fronts of these 2 sts and knit them together

k2 tog

Barranco

BACK & FRONT (One piece)
Using smaller ndles, cast on 64 (68, 72, 76, 80, 84) sts and work 2in/5cm in garter st. Change to larger ndles and cont in st st to end, casting on 11 (11, 13, 13, 15, 15) sts at beg of row using cable cast on and at end of row using backward loop cast on – 86 (90. 98, 102, 110, 114) sts. When work measures 17 (17, 17.5, 17.5, 18, 18)in/43 (43, 44.5, 44.5, 45.75, 45.75)cm from c.o.e. ending on WS row, **work neck:**

Next row (RS) Work 26 (28, 31, 33, 36, 38) sts, break yarn and place 34 (34, 36, 36, 38, 38) sts on holder, rejoin yarn to rem sts and work to end.

Next row (WS) Work 26 (28, 31, 33, 36, 38) sts, cast on 34 (34, 36, 36, 38, 38) sts by provisional cast-on method, work to end.

Cont in st st until work measures 32 (32, 33, 33, 34, 34)in/81.25 (81.25, 84, 84, 86.5, 86.5)cm from c.o.e, ending on WS row, casting off 11 (11, 13, 13, 15, 15) sts purlwise at beg of final row. Change to smaller ndles and work 2in/5cm in garter st, casting off 11 (11, 13, 13, 15, 15) sts at beg of first row – 64 (68, 72, 76, 80, 84) sts Cast off.

FINISHING
With RS facing and using circular ndle, pick up 34 (34, 36, 36, 38, 38) sts from holder at centre front and place 34 (34, 36, 36, 38, 38) sts on ndle from provisional cast-on by carefully removing the crochet and placing the live sts on ndle – 68 (68, 72, 72, 76, 76) sts. Purl 1 row to form fold line, then cont in st st (all rows k in the round), as foll:

Next round   m1, k32 (32, 34, 34, 36, 36) sts, (m1) twice, k32 (32, 34, 34, 36, 36) sts, m1

Next round   m1, k34 (34, 36, 36, 38, 38) sts, (m1) twice, k34 (34, 36, 36, 38, 38) sts, m1

Cont inc as set on every round until 6 rounds have been worked 92 (92, 96, 96, 100, 100) sts
Cast off loosely, on larger ndles or using crochet cast off to ensure sts are not too tight.
Turn neck facing to inside and stitch in place using invisible hemming stitch.

Armbands
Fold sweater in two along shoulder and measure 7.5 (7.5, 7.5, 8, 8, 8)in/19 (19, 19, 20.25, 20.25, 20. 25)cm down front and back and mark. Using smaller ndles, with RS facing and working between markers, pick up and k52 (52, 52, 56, 56, 56) sts. Work 1.5in/3.75cm in garter st and then cast off loosely.
Join side seams (vertical and horizontal edges) in one line using a slipstitch for welts and small neat backstitch on edge of work for rest of seam.

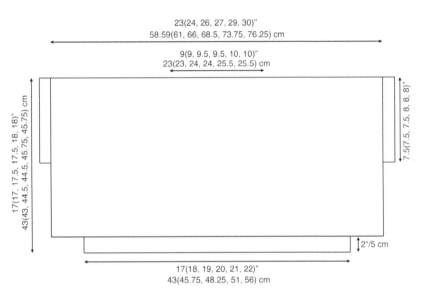

23(24, 26, 27, 29, 30)"
58.59(61, 66, 68.5, 73.75, 76.25) cm

9(9, 9.5, 9.5, 10, 10)"
23(23, 24, 24, 25.5, 25.5) cm

7.5(7.5, 7.5, 8, 8, 8)"

17(17, 17.5, 17.5, 18, 18)"
43(43, 44.5, 44.5, 45.75, 45.75) cm

2"/5 cm

17(18, 19, 20, 21, 22)"
43(45.75, 48.25, 51, 56) cm

Atacama

SIZES

S   to fit bust 32-36in/
    81.25-91.5cm

M   to fit bust 36-40in/
    91.5-101.5cm

L   to fit bust 40-44in/
    101.5-111.5cm

See schematic for actual
measurements

MATERIALS

Araucania Chacabuco:
6 (6, 6, 7, 7, 8) skeins
PT733/KFI-758
One pair 5.5mm (US 9)
needles *or size to obtain
tension*
5mm (US 8) and 5.5mm (US 9)
circular needles
4.5mm crochet hook (US H-8)
1 safety pin
99yds/90m x 0.125in/3mm silk
ribbon

TENSION

14 sts and 24 rows =
4in/10cms over garter stitch
when pressed

STITCHES

Garter stitch (in the round)
Row 1   k
Row 2   p
Repeat these 2 rows
1 x 1 rib (in the round)
*k1, p1, re from * a round

MAIN PIECE

Using straight ndles, cast on 56 (60, 64) sts
and work in garter st throughout. When
work measures 20.5 (22.5, 24.5)in/52 (57,
62.25)cm when slightly stretched, work slit
for sleeve as follows:
Work 15 (16, 17) sts, cast off 26 (28, 30) sts,
work to end. Cast on these sts when you
come to them on next row.
Cont until work measures 33.5 (36.5,
39.5)in/85 (92.75, 100.5)cm when slightly
stretched, then work another slit as above.
Cont until work measures 54 (59, 64)in/137
(149.5, 162.5)cm when slightly stretched,
then cast off.

MAIN PIECE

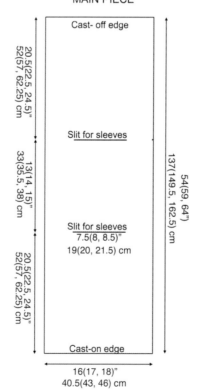

Cast- off edge

20.5(22.5, 24.5)"
52(57, 62.25) cm

Slit for sleeves

13(14, 15)"
33(35.5, 38) cm

54(59, 64")
137(149.5, 162.5) cm

Slit for sleeves
7.5(8, 8.5)"
19(20, 21.5) cm

20.5(22.5, 24.5)"
52(57, 62.25) cm

Cast-on edge

16(17, 18)"
40.5(43, 46) cm

SLEEVES

With RS facing and using larger circular
ndle, pick up and k52 (56, 60) sts around
slit for sleeve. Work in garter st for
16.75in/42.5 cm when slightly stretched,
then change to smaller ndles and work a
further 1.25in/3cm in 1 x 1 rib. Cast off.

FINISHING

Work 2 rounds of double crochet around
edge of cardigan, starting and finishing at
centre back neck. Work one round of
double crochet around each cuff.

Work flower to fasten cardigan
Using smaller ndles cast on 10 sts.

Row 1	k1
Row 2	p
Row 3	k into front and back of every st – 20 sts
Row 4	p
Row 5	k into front and back of every st – 40 sts
Row 6	p
Row 7	k into front and back of every st – 80 sts
Row 8	p

Cast off
Twist rose into spiral and sew in place on
WS. Attach bead or button in centre and
safety pin on WS.

SLEEVES

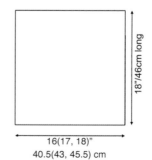

18"/46cm long

16(17, 18)"
40.5(43, 45.5) cm

USEFUL INFORMATION

SIZING
Figures in parentheses relate to S, M, L, XL and XXL sizes respectively. When there is only one figure, this relates to all.

YARN
Please note the yarn weights recommended are approximate.

As Araucania cotton is hand-dyed with no dye lots, to assure an overall blended effect, work with two hanks, changing hanks every two to four rows.

STITCHES
Slip the first stitch and knit into the back of the last stitch on every row. This eliminates a certain amount of curl and makes finishing easier as the resulting notches can be matched. NB There is no selvedge allowance in the patterns.

Garter stitch
Knit every row

Stocking stitch
Knit on RS rows, purl on WS rows

Reverse stocking stitch
Purl on RS row and knit on WS row

Moss (or seed) stitch
Row 1   *k1, p1; repeat from * to end
Row 2   knit the purl sts and purl the knit stitches
Repeat row 2

1 x 1 rib
*k1, p1, rep across 1st row; on subsequent rows keep knit and purl sts correct.

1 x 1 rib (in the round)
Round 1 *k1, p1, repeat from * around
Repeat this round.

K2, p2 rib
Row 1   k2, *p2, k2; rep from * to end
Row 2   p2, *k2, p2; rep from * to end

CASTING ON
I usually use the thumb method since, like the continental cast-on, it gives an elastic edge. If you have a tendency to cast on tightly then also use a needle one or two sizes larger than what the pattern calls for. For cast-on stitches in middle of a row, I use a cable cast-on.

Cable cast-on
Make a slip knot on the left needle. Working into this knot's loop, knit a stitch and place it on left needle. *Insert right needle between last two stitches. From this position knit a stitch and place it on left needle. Repeat from * for each additional stitch.

Provisional cast-on
Using waste yarn make a slip knot loop on the crochet hook. Note that this loop does not become a stitch. Holding the knitting needle in your left hand, and the crochet hook in your right hand, bring the yarn behind the needle. Bring the crochet hook in front of the needle and pick up the yarn. Pull a loop through the loop on the crochet hook – there is 1 cast-on stitch on the knitting needle. Take the yarn back behind the needle and repeat this process until you have the desired number of stitches cast on. Break the yarn and pull a large loop through the last loop on the crochet hook. Don't tie off - this is the end from which you will unravel the chain to recapture the stitches. When you need the live stitches at the cast-on edge, gently pull out the chain and place each stitch on needle.

CASTING OFF
I use the basic chain cast-off and always cast off in pattern, keeping knit, purl, yarn overs, decreases etc correct. If you cast off on the wrong side, this will hide the chain edge. For projects like shawls or those which require the cast-on and cast-off edges to be the same width, the important thing to bear in mind is that it's often better to cast off using needles at least one size larger, especially if you have a tendency to knit tightly. Casting off using a crochet hook also helps solve this problem as you can more easily regulate the length of the stitches.

TENSION

Always work a tension swatch measuring at least 6 in/15 cm square. If your tension is incorrect, then the size of the finished garment will also be incorrect. Calculate your tension as follows:

Divide number of **stitches** *by* **width** of swatch
Divide number of **rows** *by* **length** of swatch
For instance, if your swatch measures 6in/15 cm x 6in/15 cm and you cast on 30 sts and worked 42 rows, you would divide 30 sts by 6in/15 cm to get 5 sts per inch, and divide 42 rows by 6in/15 cm to get 7 rows per inch. Therefore your tension would be **5 sts and 7 rows per inch**. If you have too many stitches per inch then try larger needles, if too few try smaller needles until you have the tension called for in the pattern.

READING KNITTING CHARTS

When knitting back and forth, charts are read from right to left on right-side rows and from left to right on wrong-side rows. Charts can begin with a right-side or wrong-side row, this will be indicated by where *row 1* is situated on the chart. For instance if *row 1* is on the left, then the chart starts with a wrong-side row, if it is on the right, it starts with a right-side row. In circular knitting all rows are right-side rows and every row is read from right to left. Every square (or rectangle) represents one stitch horizontally and one row vertically. The symbols represent either stitches (knit, purl, cable etc) or colours (in intarsia or two-colour stranded knitting).

FINISHING

First, neaten selvedges by sewing/weaving in all the ends along sides or along colour joins where appropriate. Then, using pins, block out each piece of knitting to shape to match dimensions on schematic. Next, gently press each piece, omitting ribs, using a warm iron over a damp cloth. Take special care with the edges, as this will make sewing up easier. Take time to pin the garment first and, before sewing, make sure you're satisfied with the way the pieces are fitting together. Keep areas of pattern and texture in line across sweater, matching the notches made by the selvedge stitches. Use a small neat backstitch on inside of the selvedge stitch for all main seams as this creates a very stable, strong seam. Join ribs and neckband with a slip stitch so that they lay flat. This method is suitable for all but bulky yarn. In this case use mattress stitch.

ABBREVIATIONS

cm(s)	centimetre(s)	patt	pattern
in(s)	inch(es)	ev	every
m	metres	beg	beginning
g	grams	rem	remaining
yd(s)	yard(s)	k2tog	knit 2 sts together
mm	millimetres	p2tog	purl 2 sts together
st(s)	stitch(es)	k3tog	knit 3 sts together
dpn(s)	double pointed needle(s)	p3tog	purl 3 sts together
WS	wrong-side	tbl	through back loop
RS	right-side	sl	slip
k	knit	psso	pass slipped stitch over
p	purl	rev st st	reverse stocking stitch
st st	stocking stitch	ssk	(slip, slip, knit): slip next 2 sts knitwise, one at a time to RH needle. Insert tip of LH needle into fronts of these sts from left to right and knit them together
no	number		
rep	repeat		
ndle(s)	needle(s)		
cn	cable needle		
cont	continue	sskpo	slip 2 sts as if to work k2tog, k1, pass two slipped stitches over
foll	following/follows		
c.o.e	cast on edge	yo	yarn over needle to make 1 st
alt	alternate	yf	yarn to front of work
dec	decrease	yb	yarn to back of work
inc	increase	yrn	yarn round needle to make a st NB knit tbl on foll row
		m1	pick up horizontal strand of yarn lying between st just worked and next st and knit into back of it
		c8f	place 4 sts on cable ndle and hold at front of work, k4, then k4 from cn
		c4f	place 2 sts on cable ndle and hold at front of work, k2, then k2 from cn
		c8b	place 4 sts on cn and hold at back of work, k4, k4 from cn
		c5f	place 3 sts on cn and hold at front of work, k2, k3 from cn
		c5b	place 2 sts on cn and hold at back of work, k3, k2 from cn

ARAUCANIA YARNS

Araucania yarns are inspired by ancient Chilean crafts and made from hand-painted natural yarns. As there are no dye lots, knit with two skeins in assorted rows to ensure an overall blended effect.

Chacabuco
100% Pima cotton
122.5yds/112m per 100g skein

Patagonia
100% cotton
105yds/100m per 100g skein

Pomaire
100% Pima cotton
183yds/168m per 100g skein

Ulmo
100% cotton
202yds/185m per 100g skein

Nature Cotton
100% cotton
105yds/100m per 100g skein

DISTRIBUTORS

For details of Araucania Yarns stockists please contact:

UK & EUROPE
Designer Yarns Ltd
Units 8-10 Newbridge Industrial Estate
Pitt Street
Keighley BD21 4PQ
P: +44 (0)1535 664222
F: +44 (0)1535 664333
E: alex@designeryarns.uk.com
www.designeryarns.uk.com

USA
Knitting Fever Inc
315 Bayview Avenue
Amityville
NY 11701
P: 001 516 546 3600
F: 001 516 546 6871
www.knittingfever.com

CANADA
Diamond Yarns Ltd
155 Martin Ross Avenue Unit 3
Toronto
Ontario M3J 2L9
P: 001 416 736 6111
F: 001 416 736 6112
www.diamondyarns.com

DENMARK
Fancy Knit
Hovedvejen 71
8586 Oerum Djurs
P: (45) 59 462189
E: roenneburg@mail.dk

BELGIUM & HOLLAND
Pavan
Meerlaanstraat 73
9860 Balegem (Oostrezele)
P: +32 (0) 9 221 85 94
E: pavan@pandora.be

SWEDEN
Hamilton Design
Storgatan 14
64730 Mariefred
P/F: +46 (0) 159 12006
www.hamiltondesign.biz

FRANCE
Elle Tricote
8 Rue du Coq
La Petite France
67000 Strasbourg
P: +33 (0) 388 230313
F: +33 (0) 8823 0169

GERMANY, AUSTRIA, SWITZERLAND & LUXEMBOURG
Designer Yarns (Deutschland) Ltd
Sachsstrasse 30
D-50259 Pulheim-Brauweiler
Germany
P: +49 (0) 2234 205453
F: +49 (0) 2234 205456
E: kk@designeryarns.de

SPAIN
Oyambre Needlework SL
Balmes
200 At. 4
08006 Barcelona
P: +34 (0) 93 487 26 72
F: +34 (0) 93 218 6694
E: info@oyambreonline.com

AUSTRALIA/NEW ZEALAND
Prestige Yarns Pty Ltd
PO Box 39
Bulli
NSW 2516
P: +61 02 4285 6669
E: infor@prestigeyarns.com
www.prestigeyarns.com

FINLAND
Duo Design
Kaikukuja 1 c 31
00530 Helsinki
P: +358 (0) 9 753 1716
E: maria.hellbom@priima.net
www.duodesign.fi